RAND NATIONAL DEFENSE RESEARCH INSTITUTE

T0288871

DoD STARBASE

Improved Measures for Participation, Outreach, and Impact

Jennie W. Wenger, Esther M. Friedman, Erin N. Leidy, Michael Vasseur, Kristin J. Leuschner

Prepared for the Office of the Secretary of Defense
Approved for public release; distribution unlimited

For more information on this publication, visit www.rand.org/t/RR2160

Library of Congress Cataloging-in-Publication Data is available for this publication.
ISBN: 978-1-9774-0104-5

Published by the RAND Corporation, Santa Monica, Calif.
© Copyright 2018 RAND Corporation
RAND® is a registered trademark.

Cover Image by Master Sgt. Bob Haskell, U.S. Air Force.

Support RAND
Make a tax-deductible charitable contribution at
www.rand.org/giving/contribute

www.rand.org

Preface

The STARBASE program provides hands-on instruction in science, technology, engineering, and math (STEM) topics to fifth graders from disadvantaged schools. Classrooms of students (with their teachers) visit the program for five days of instruction and hands-on activities. RAND was asked by the Office of the Assistant Secretary of Defense for Manpower and Reserve Affairs to provide a description of who participates, analyze current outreach efforts, and develop additional measures of outreach for the program.

First we examine, through several measures of school and neighborhood disadvantage, the characteristics of neighborhoods and schools where STARBASE programs are situated. Using directors' reports and other published data, we characterize the program's current outreach efforts. We also examine the role STARBASE has in the participation footprint of all Department of Defense (DoD) youth programs, including the Junior Reserve Officers' Training Corps (JROTC) and National Guard Youth ChalleNGe. Finally we suggest several potential ways to measure the outreach and influence of STARBASE and other DoD youth programs. We focus on direct outreach efforts from STARBASE programs, on documenting the footprint created by DoD's youth programs, and on considering ways in which these youth programs could influence longer-term outcomes, such as the number and quality of military applicants or overall attitudes toward the military. We caution that our analyses of longer-term outcomes should be seen as exploratory in nature.

This research was sponsored by the Office of the Assistant Secretary of Defense for Reserve Affairs (Resources) and conducted within the Forces and Resources Policy Center of the RAND Corporation's National Defense Research Institute, a federally funded research and development center sponsored by the Office of the Secretary of Defense, the Joint Staff, the Unified Combatant Commands, the Department of the Navy, the Marine Corps, U.S. defense agencies, and the defense intelligence community. For more information on RAND Forces and Resources Policy Center, see www.rand.org/nsrd/ndri/centers/frp or contact the director (contact information is provided on the web page).

Questions and comments regarding this research are welcome and should be directed to the leaders of the research team: Jennie W. Wenger (Jennie_Wenger@rand.org) or Esther Friedman (Esther_Friedman@rand.org).

Contents

Figures

Tables

Summary

The Department of Defense's STARBASE program offers an innovative curriculum focused on science, technology, engineering, and mathematics (STEM) for students in underserved areas of the United States. First started in 1991, STARBASE now has 59 programs across 31 states and Puerto Rico. Its mission is to provide 25 hours of high-quality hands-on instruction and activities, and the goals of the program are to "expose our nation's youth to the technological environments and positive civilian and military role models found on Active, Guard, and Reserve military bases and installations, nurture a winning network of collaborators, and build mutual loyalty within our communities."[1] On the individual level, the program serves to improve STEM knowledge, particularly in the disadvantaged student population. At the community level, STARBASE's goal is to serve as an outreach program, improving community relations and building mutual loyalty and feelings of goodwill between communities and the Department of Defense (DoD).

To accomplish these objectives, the STARBASE program serves fifth graders from disadvantaged schools; classrooms of students (and their teachers) participate in a week of hands-on activities as part of STARBASE's STEM-focused curriculum. Activities generally occur on military bases or installations; certified teachers run the classrooms at STARBASE programs, while military volunteers assist by leading tours, visiting classrooms, and providing examples of STEM-relevant military careers and applications. Along with providing STEM-based educational opportunities, STARBASE also seeks to build positive ties in communities.

Previous research suggests that STARBASE is quite effective on a variety of short- and long-term outcome measures, including student test scores and student reports of confidence or efficacy on STEM subjects, as well as longer-term outcomes, such as encouraging interest in technology, lowering school absences, and improving scores on standardized tests. To date, however, less is known about how effective the program is at targeting disadvantaged students, and very little is known about whether STARBASE achieves its goals as a community outreach program. Indeed, there is no

---

[1] See dodstarbase.org, accessed March 23, 2017.

consensus on how to measure outreach efforts and outcomes from STARBASE or other similar programs.

The Focus of This Study

Because of these deficits, and because outreach is central to the program's mission, this study focuses on the students served and the program's outreach efforts. Specifically, we examine four research questions:

1. What communities are served by STARBASE, and is the program reaching the disadvantaged populations it is designed to reach?
2. What are the direct outreach efforts employed by STARBASE program directors, and how might they build awareness of the program?
3. What other paths could serve as indirect methods of program outreach and influence—that is, how might STARBASE build positive perceptions of the military or positive sentiments toward the military?
4. What are some examples of potential measures that could capture the impact of outreach efforts from questions 2 and 3, above?

Outreach is a difficult concept to define and an even harder one to measure. In our search of the literature on youth-based community outreach efforts, we found very few established metrics for measuring outreach and its longer-term outcomes. In this report we therefore take a broad view of outreach and consider both direct, active outreach efforts (e.g., direct advertisement and publicity of a program) and indirect or more passive efforts (e.g., local program presence) through which an outreach program can less directly and maybe even less consciously exert influence.[2]

To address the research questions above, we begin by examining the population characteristics of those served by the STARBASE program: Do they differ from populations not served by these efforts and, if so, are these differences consistent with the program's mission of outreach? Next we turn to direct outreach efforts, primarily those on the part of STARBASE program directors. We follow this with an examination of measures of indirect program outreach and influence—including, for example, geographic placement of the programs. That is, we look at residential proximity to a program to see if just living near to a program can have *indirect* or spillover effects and thereby have an even greater effect on communities. Finally, we examine two possible consequences of these outreach efforts that capture positive attitudes toward the military, and increased numbers of applicants or accessions into the military. The methods used and findings of our investigations are summarized briefly below.

---

[2]   We use the terms *outreach* and *influence* interchangeably in the text to refer to indirect/passive outreach efforts.

Communities Served by STARBASE

STARBASE is designed to reach disadvantaged fifth graders and provide opportunities for these students to experience an interactive STEM curriculum. The program serves Title I schools, which have a high concentration of students who come from low-income families (it should be noted that about half of public schools are categorized as Title I). To answer our first research question, we examined the characteristics of communities served by STARBASE. We compiled several sources of community and school data and found that STARBASE was reaching the most disadvantaged communities on many measures: overall socioeconomic disadvantage, crime rates, and the percentage of the population categorized as racial/ethnic minorities—a group that is typically disadvantaged when it comes to participation in STEM. These communities are the ones in greatest need of STEM outreach.[3] Existing STARBASE programs are frequently located in relatively large districts, which suggests that the programs have the potential to serve many additional students without expanding into new districts.

Direct Outreach from STARBASE Directors

As mentioned above, one of the goals of the program is to foster outreach. The most straightforward way to think about outreach is to consider the direct efforts to foster awareness of a program among an intended population; such efforts generally are made by the administrative staff of a given program. In the case of the STARBASE program, it is the individual program directors who seek to foster this type of relationship with the community. The STARBASE directors report building relationships with a wide variety of local organizations, including youth programs and colleges and universities that could be important sources of information on current STEM curriculum and/or potential partners to provide other resources (such as guest speakers to talk about STEM-related careers). We also discovered several hundred newspaper stories about STARBASE that were published in local papers during the last decade. We do not know whether these stories were placed by program directors or written by local reporters, but in either case, these represent potential outreach and influence. While we have no measure of the *effectiveness* of these efforts, they have the potential to improve community relations and create or improve positive impressions of the military among the general population.

We also explored the extent to which STARBASE programs use social media as an outreach tool. For STARBASE, the primary existing social media efforts occur at the program level: individual sites frequently have Facebook pages. However, those pages have relatively low levels of traffic. Using Google Trends data, we also found

---

[3]   A variety of scholars have examined groups most disadvantaged when it comes to STEM from a number of perspectives; see, for example, Margolis et al. (2008).

low levels of relevant searches related to STARBASE. These findings could be reflective of the STARBASE audience's internet use; fifth graders and their parents may seek information in other ways. We have no evidence that encouraging individual STARBASE sites to make a larger investment in social media outreach efforts would pay off. Another option would be to focus resources on providing information about STARBASE to the broader public, perhaps as part of a larger outreach effort.

Indirect Measures of Program Influence and Outreach

In this section we focus on efforts to build positive perceptions or sentiments toward the military through the STARBASE program. We address these research questions in several ways. One indirect pathway through which STARBASE's (and other military programs') influence could occur is through the mere presence of a program. Such presence of a program could create positive perceptions of the military by serving as part of the military's institutional presence, particularly if the program is located in an area not already served by other military programs. To examine this, we carried out a geographic analysis of STARBASE along with DoD's other youth programs: National Guard Youth ChalleNGe and the Junior Reserve Officers' Training Corps (JROTC). While JROTC is much larger in size than either STARBASE or ChalleNGe, we found that all three programs have the potential to add to DoD's indirect outreach efforts based on location. Nearly one-third of ChalleNGe programs, and the majority of STARBASE programs, are located in districts with no other military youth outreach efforts. In general, our analyses suggest that DoD's youth programs are often positioned in a way that could maximize outreach effectiveness by filling in gap areas without other sources of military influence.

Potential Outcomes from Outreach Efforts

Together, the outreach efforts described above could result in longer-term positive effects on behaviors and attitudes toward STARBASE, its subject matter (STEM), and the military more generally. There are no established metrics for capturing these longer-term effects of military outreach efforts such as STARBASE; we thus explored potential related measures, such as the number and quality of applicants and accessions to the military, as well as public attitudes toward the armed forces.

Our results indicate that districts with DoD youth programs have more military applicants than would be expected, even after correcting for a variety of other factors; this result holds for urban and suburban areas with STARBASE programs, though not for rural areas. We also found that there are more accessions in suburban districts with DoD youth programs than would be expected. Our results also indicate that, in some areas, the presence of a military base is correlated with applicants and accessions.

Analysis of data from the General Social Survey (GSS) shows that confidence in the military has been on the rise in the United States when compared to confidence in other governmental institutions. These data provide a potentially relevant measure of the effectiveness of the military's outreach programs (though confidence in the military is surely influenced by other factors, such as world events). Unfortunately, the measure is available only at the state (versus more local) level. Across the board, we found that DoD youth programs are located in states with relatively high levels of trust in the military, but in the cases of STARBASE and ChalleNGe, this is less common. The difference in trust between states with and without these programs is small, but some of the programs are located in areas with relatively low levels of trust in the military. In this sense, at least some STARBASE and ChalleNGe programs may be well located to create positive outreach and improve confidence in the military.

We caution that these outcome measures and analyses should be seen as exploratory. We use them to demonstrate the types of outreach measures that could be developed to capture the long-term impact of outreach efforts. It was beyond the scope of this study to examine these outcomes using a true experimental (causal) design, but these findings suggest that these measures could be promising avenues for future work. We will turn to a discussion of possible next steps for capturing and analyzing outcomes below.

Expanding Outreach Efforts to Influencers Through Social Media

Because social media is becoming a key basis of many outreach efforts, we reviewed existing data on how influencers (family members and others in the community who are thought to have influence over young people's decisions about education, careers, and the like) use it. We find that social media is viewed as a relatively trustworthy source of information, and one that is likely to become increasingly relevant in the future as it becomes a more prevalent way of conveying information. Influencers engaging with online DoD content tend to be comfortable with the DoD and military service (e.g., they are more willing to recommend military service and report higher levels of knowledge of the military than are other influencers). While we find that social media is not currently a major source of influencer impressions of the military, it is expanding as a source of information faster than any other type of media, suggesting that it could become an increasingly valuable avenue for future outreach efforts, especially as today's youth transition into roles as influencers.

Recommendations and Next Steps

The STARBASE program reaches a substantial number of students in Title I schools; these students' communities face substantial disadvantages. In this sense the program is functioning as it was designed. Regardless of future expansion, future tracking of the levels of disadvantage among the students and communities served will provide a way to document the extent to which the STARBASE program continues to serve students from disadvantaged schools.

Based on the findings of this research, we also make the following recommendations:

Explore the use of increased social media outreach for DoD youth programs. Currently, STARBASE programs have very modest social media outreach efforts, mostly run by individual programs through Facebook accounts. A centralized social media campaign could have the potential to increase awareness of and support for STARBASE, and potentially for other DoD programs. While the literature on social media is still quite nascent, there is persuasive evidence, especially from the health field, that social media can be an effective method of outreach. Of course, the cost of such a centralized campaign should be weighed against other investments. That said, a campaign that focuses more broadly on STEM education resources for students in grades five through 12 could also offer a way to keep STARBASE graduates engaged through middle school and high school. Teachers may be the best group to target with such a campaign; despite the availability of STEM resources online, teachers who have attended STARBASE indicate that they use STARBASE materials in their classrooms. A campaign focusing more generally on STEM (versus specifically on STARBASE) could also yield greater returns. But a wider campaign focused on influencers could also be a sensible approach; such a campaign could also include DoD's other youth programs. We suggest that any social media effort related to STARBASE should be run centrally (rather than allocating responsibility to individual programs). And again, such a campaign's costs should be weighed against other potential sources of positive outreach.

Centrally manage DoD's youth programs. Measuring outreach efforts poses a substantial challenge. Our results represent a first step in measuring the effectiveness of DoD's youth programs outreach, but more work is necessary to develop and test appropriate measures of outreach and their long-term impact. If the youth programs are considered as a group, placement decisions could be made to maximize both access to the programs and potential outreach. In general, our results suggest that separating youth programs from other outreach efforts could yield positive results.

Work toward a better understanding of the relationships between youth programs, military institutional presence, and the public's perceptions of DoD. Establishing improved measures of outreach could assist DoD in measuring the extent to which youth programs achieve this aspect of their missions. Our results indicate that there are more applicants, and sometimes more accessions, in areas with youth programs, although our study design does not enable us to establish this relationship as causal. In addition, existing STARBASE and ChalleNGe programs appear to be placed in areas with lower levels of military confidence than areas that have JROTC programs.

One method of measuring effectiveness in building positive perceptions of the military would be to conduct a survey of a random subsample of the population, asking questions about awareness and impressions of various aspects of military outreach programs. Another potentially more cost-effective approach would be to adapt an existing survey for this purpose. While the GSS that we utilize is fairly small in scope, it is possible that additional analyses with this data source could produce valuable information about the factors that influence military confidence, and especially those factors related to changes in the public's confidence in the military. Because our analyses of access to youth programs and military confidence was at the state level, it was beyond the scope of this work to do a thorough investigation into the individual-level factors that are related to military confidence. The Youth Poll and Influencer Poll of DoD's Joint Advertising Market Research & Studies (JAMRS) program could also provide useful information. We do note that the STARBASE program currently surveys students and teachers; results indicate that participants do, in the short term, develop more positive perceptions of the military (Wenger, Huff, and Schulte, 2013); the other suggestions above would be relevant for determining how this program, or how DoD's outreach programs, influence the general public.

Acknowledgments

Several of our RAND colleagues have made valuable contributions to this effort. We are grateful to Christine Peterson for her assistance with cleaning and merging data from several sources, and to Eric Larson for developing the outreach model featured in the report and for contributing to the report's overall organization. We also appreciate the contributions of Cynthia Christopher, Katharine Sieck, and Douglas Yeung. We thank our reviewers, Scott Hughes of the University of New Mexico and John Pane of the RAND Corporation; their comments strengthened this document and helped to ensure that our work met RAND's high standards for quality. Our RAND colleagues, Craig Bond and John Winkler, also read portions of the report and provided helpful feedback. We thank all who assisted with this report, but we retain full responsibility for the accuracy, objectivity, and analytical integrity of the work presented here.

Some of the data used in these analyses are derived from the National Center for Education Statistics (NCES) Common Core of Data Local Education Agency completer data files, obtained under contractual arrangements to protect the anonymity of those included in the files. These data are *not* available from the authors; persons interested in obtaining these files should contact the NCES.

Some of the data used in these analyses are derived from Sensitive Data Files of the GSS, obtained under special contractual arrangements designed to protect the anonymity of respondents. These data are *not* available from the authors; persons interested in obtaining these files should contact the GSS at GSS@NORC.org.

Abbreviations

ACS   American Community Survey

CCD   Common Core of Data

DoD   Department of Defense

GSS   General Social Survey

JAMRS   Joint Advertising Market Research & Studies

JROTC   Junior Reserve Officers' Training Corps

NCES   National Center for Education Statistics

STEM   science, technology, engineering, and mathematics

CHAPTER ONE

STARBASE: Background, Prior Research

The Department of Defense (DoD) STARBASE program offers curriculum focused on science, technology, engineering, and mathematics (STEM) to students in underserved areas. First started in 1991 at a single site, STARBASE now has 59 programs across 31 states and Puerto Rico. The goals of STARBASE are well described in the program's vision and mission statements:

> *Vision Statement.* To be the premier Department of Defense youth outreach program for raising the interest in learning and improving the knowledge and skills of our nation's at-risk youth so that we may develop a highly educated and skilled American workforce who can meet the advance technological requirements of the Department of Defense.

> *Mission Statement.* To expose our nation's youth to the technological environments and positive civilian and military role models found on Active, Guard, and Reserve military bases and installations, nurture a winning network of collaborators, and build mutual loyalty within our communities, by providing 25 hours of exemplary hands-on instruction and activities that meet or exceed the National Standards. (Department of Defense STARBASE, "Vision and Mission," undated)

To accomplish these objectives, the STARBASE program serves fifth graders from schools that qualify for Title I funds. Classrooms of students (and their teachers) are invited to participate in a week of hands-on activities as part of STARBASE's STEM-focused curriculum. Activities generally occur on military bases or installations; professional instructors run the classrooms at STARBASE programs, while military volunteers assist by leading tours, visiting classrooms, and providing examples of STEM-relevant military careers and applications.

Along with providing STEM-based educational opportunities, STARBASE also seeks to build positive ties in communities. Accordingly, as is the case with DoD's other youth programs, such as National Guard Youth ChalleNGe and the Junior Reserve Officers' Training Corps (JROTC), STARBASE is designed to improve opportunities for young people *and* to conduct outreach to local communities that have school districts hosting the programs. For all of these programs, then, a primary purpose is to create positive bonds in communities (as expressed in the STARBASE mission statement). As Secretary of Defense Ash Carter has noted,

> We're going to try to better leverage our most successful outreach programs and also help—[those] that already help people give back to America's communities. One example is called STARBASE, where our servicemembers volunteer in local elementary schools and help inspire kids to explore and learn more about science, technology, engineering and math. And that allows us to help them, but also allows those little kids to get to know us in a hands-on way, and we want to have more of that opportunity in both directions. (Carter, 2016)

These remarks indicate the importance of STARBASE as a form of positive community outreach and suggest that the program might be expected to have impacts well beyond the academic achievement of those who participate in it.

Previous research suggests that STARBASE is quite effective on a variety of short- and long-term outcome measures. Participants' scores on a test aligned with the STARBASE curriculum are substantially higher at the end of the program than at the beginning; STARBASE participants also show improvements in confidence or efficacy on STEM subjects, and have more positive views of the military at the end of the program.[1] But there is also evidence of positive effects on longer-term outcomes, including levels of interest in technology, and in lowering school absences and improving scores on standardized tests.[2] However, to date there has been little focus in the existing research on the potential outreach effects of STARBASE, including impacts on the broader community beyond the specific students who have engaged in the program. Because of this deficit, and because outreach is central to the program's mission (and to the missions of other DoD youth programs), the current study focuses on the effectiveness of the program at targeting disadvantaged communities and on measures of outreach efforts and possible outcomes from such program efforts.

The Purpose of This Study

This study begins to address this gap by examining what is known about STARBASE's role as a community outreach program, including the characteristics of the communities it serves, and by developing and testing a variety of measures to assess outreach and potential outcomes of outreach. We organize our analyses around four broad questions:

1. What communities are served by STARBASE, and is the program reaching the disadvantaged populations it is designed to reach?

---

[1]   See DoD STARBASE (2015); and Wenger, Huff, and Schulte, (2013).

[2]   Differences on other academic outcomes were generally not statistically significant (and thus could have occurred by chance), but were in the expected direction. See Dauphinee et al. (2015); and Sharpe Solutions (2015).

2. What are the direct outreach efforts employed by STARBASE program directors?
3. What other paths could serve as indirect methods of program outreach and influence?
4. What are some examples of potential measures that could capture the impact of outreach efforts from questions 2 and 3, above?

Outreach is a hard concept to define and an even harder one to measure. In our search of the literature on youth-based community outreach efforts, we found very few established metrics for measuring outreach and its longer-term outcomes. While there is very little research on the effectiveness of broad military outreach efforts, there are studies that focus on specific aspects of military outreach.[3] In many cases, they focus on recruiting and on geographic access to recruiters.[4] The sociological literature includes some references to the *military institutional presence*; this concept was developed by Burk (2001) as a mechanism to explain how the military has maintained influence as an institution, even as its presence has diminished on some measures such as relative spending and total number of bases.[5] For studying the reach and influence of the STARBASE program, we take a broad view of outreach that incorporates direct and active outreach efforts (e.g., direct advertisement and publicity of a program), as well as indirect or more passive mechanisms (e.g., local program presence) through which an outreach program can less directly and maybe even less consciously exert influence.[6] The indirect methods are developed building on work by Burk (2001), and include, among other things, program presence. We were interested both in current outreach efforts and opportunities to expand outreach in the future.

To address the first research question, we examine the population characteristics of those served by the STARBASE program: Do they differ from populations not served by these efforts, and, if so, is it in ways that are consistent with the program's mission of outreach?

For research questions 2 and 3, we posit that the STARBASE program could have positive outreach effects or exert influence through a variety of mechanisms. We argue that there are two broad pathways through which program influence may occur. First, direct outreach efforts of individual programs could create a positive sense of the

[3] While there is a well-developed literature on community outreach efforts, much of it focuses on efforts that are unrelated to the STARBASE program, such as efforts to improve public health measures; the literature generally focuses on the extent to which programs raise general awareness.

[4] See, e.g., Orvis et al. (2016).

[5] Kleykamp (2006) uses the concept of institutional presence to explain the decisions high school seniors make between work, college, and enlistment. She develops a measure of military presence based on the percentage of employment at the county level that is made up of active duty military members. This measure focuses on one aspect of Burk's definition, albeit the aspect that may have the largest influence on community outreach. Kleykamp finds that this measure does help to explain enlistment decision.

[6] We use the terms *outreach* and *influence* interchangeably in the text to refer to indirect/passive outreach efforts.

military's impact on their immediate communities. We explore this possibility by examining STARBASE directors' reported outreach efforts at the individual program level.

A second possibility is that the mere *presence* of the program could create positive outreach in a manner that might not be well captured by directors' reported outreach efforts. In other words, the program could form part of the military's *institutional presence* and thereby increase positive outreach even for people who do not benefit directly from the program or who otherwise would have little interaction with the military. Examples would include members of the public who learn about STARBASE from publicity or from participants and teachers who spend the week on a military base with a class.

The direct and indirect outreach efforts examined as part of research questions 2 and 3 could result in longer-term positive outcomes. There are many potential outcomes that could capture behaviors and attitudes toward STARBASE, its subject matter (STEM), and the military more generally. While there are no established metrics for capturing the extent to which STARBASE (or other similar programs) influence attitudes toward the military, we examine two possible types of measures to demonstrate the types of outreach measures that could be developed to capture the long-term impact of outreach efforts: the number and quality of applicants and military accessions, and public attitudes toward the military. These capture two very different types of outcomes that could conceivably occur from exposure to DoD youth programs. The first addresses direct military engagement through application or accession, while the second takes a subtler form by increasing positive feelings toward the military even if it does not influence someone to join the armed forces. We stress that these are only two of many potential measures; for example, the DoD hires substantial numbers of STEM-trained civilians, so attitudes or intentions toward STEM careers in DoD could serve as another potential measure. Indeed, these outcome measures and analyses should be seen as exploratory. It is beyond the scope of this study to examine these outcomes using a true experimental (causal) design, but these findings suggest that these measures could be promising avenues for future work. We return to a discussion of possible next steps for capturing and analyzing outcomes of outreach in Chapter Seven. In the remainder of this introduction we provide further background information about the STARBASE program, including trends in participation and costs and research on program effectiveness.

STARBASE Program Structure and Trends in Participation and Cost

Since its inception in 1991, STARBASE has served over 1 million students at a cost to DoD of about $350 per student (DoD STARBASE, 2015).[7] In recent years, many sites have also added an after-school program aimed at middle school students, STARBASE 2.0.

---

[7]   The $350 is DoD's total program cost per student. This includes costs for STARBASE 2.0 (the after-school version of STARBASE for students in middle schools), but STARBASE 2.0 costs make up a small proportion of the total costs. Transportation costs, which are paid for by the school districts, are not included in the $350 figure.

STARBASE provides approximately 25 hours of STEM-focused instruction to fifth graders; their teachers also attend, but are not responsible for instruction during the program. The program provides additional supplemental materials for teachers to use in continuing to explore in their classrooms the subjects introduced during STARBASE. In some cases, STARBASE classes meet one day per week for five weeks; in many cases, classes meet for five consecutive days in a single week. In either case, schools or districts are responsible for transporting students to the STARBASE site, while the program provides all the necessary materials and instruction.

STARBASE has grown fairly steadily since the pilot program began. Figure 1.1 shows the number of participants and the (inflation-adjusted) cost per participant over the last 12 years (comparable data are not readily available for earlier years). In 2014 the number of students participating decreased, and, consequentially, the cost per student increased, due to a sudden decrease in the number of programs; however, the number of participants and cost per student have since returned to trend.

It is not clear how best to benchmark the costs of STARBASE; the program is somewhat unique among enrichment programs (many of which run after school or in the summer months). Therefore, we offer several potentially relevant measures. First, the current per-pupil expenditure for public elementary and secondary students was $11,568 in FY2015 (Cornman et al., 2017).[8] This figure equates to about $320 per week. Another potential point of comparison is the cost of after-school enrichment programs; those programs that can be considered of high quality generally have a cost of about $8 per hour per participant, or roughly $250 per week (Grossman et al., 2009).[9] Based on these very rough calculations, the STARBASE program appears to have costs that are not radically higher than other programs especially when considering the technological resources and small student-to-teacher ratio that is provided.

Based on the number of hours of instruction, the STARBASE program might be expected to have, at most, small impacts. However, other "small dosage" programs have been found to influence student outcomes.[10] And in the case of STARBASE, teachers can attend annually, so many are exposed to the program repeatedly; this provides another potential pathway for STARBASE to influence the quality of STEM instruction.[11] Finally, the after-school STARBASE 2.0 programs may further influence students who participate.

---

[8] The figure is inflated to 2016 dollars.

[9] The figure is inflated to 2016 dollars.

[10] See, e.g., Walton and Cohen (2007). For a discussion of a series of effective interventions, see Dweck, Walton, and Cohen (2014).

[11] Past analyses suggest that teachers do use materials and information gained in the classroom, and that teachers in states with relatively weak educational standards are more likely than others to use the materials (DoD STARBASE, 2014; Wenger, Huff, and Schulte, 2013). Also, teachers report recommending STARBASE to others (DoD STARBASE, 2014).

Figure 1.1
Trends in STARBASE Participants, Costs

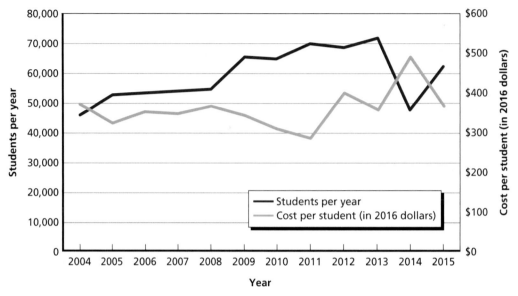

SOURCE: Authors' calculations based on STARBASE *Annual Reports*, various years.
RAND RR2160OSD-1.1

The STARBASE program is designed to provide instructional opportunities for disadvantaged students; for this reason, the program serves students in Title I schools.[12] There are about 3.7 million fifth graders in U.S. schools today; more than 2 million of these students attend Title I schools (see Figure 1.2). This suggests that there are many fifth graders who are eligible to take part in STARBASE.

Given sufficient resources and need, there is room to expand STARBASE's reach. When we tabulate only students who attend Title I schools in districts that are *currently* served by STARBASE, we find that there are roughly 250,000 such fifth graders in U.S. public schools (see Figure 1.2). STARBASE currently serves roughly 60,000 students per year. This suggests that existing STARBASE programs serve about one-fourth of the Title I students in relevant school districts. Of course, some schools may opt out of STARBASE, and some districts may be large enough to make travel time prohibitive from some schools; in this sense, our measure may overestimate the number of students in relevant districts who practicably could participate in

---

[12] Schools with a concentration of low-income students qualify for Title I funds. Currently, about half of elementary schools are classified as Title I, and slightly over half of all fifth graders attend a Title I school. Authors' calculations, based on the National Center for Education Statistics (NCES), Common Core of Data (CCD); data available at NCES, CCD (undated).

Figure 1.2
Fifth Graders, Title I Schools, STARBASE

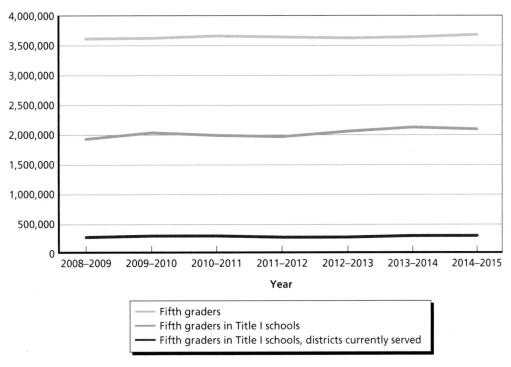

SOURCE: Authors' calculations, based on NCES, CCD, undated.
RAND RR2160OSD-1.2

STARBASE.[13] But overall, this calculation suggests that, while STARBASE programs already serve a substantial proportion of the Title I students in the districts with existing programs, STARBASE could serve additional students without opening new locations.

Prior Research on STARBASE Program Effectiveness

Many programs and interventions focus on disadvantaged students, and concerns about the quality of STEM education are not new.[14] STARBASE has important

---

[13] The Los Angeles Unified School District, which serves over 600,000 students and covers over 700 square miles, is an extreme example of this, but some rural districts are very large as well; examples include districts in Alaska. Finally, Hawaii's schools, spread across its many islands, are organized in a single school district. In each of these cases, travel across the district to attend a program in a single school day is likely to be impractical.

[14] Concerns about STEM education are commonly traced back to 1957, when the Soviet Union launched the first satellite into orbit. In response, the United States provided substantial additional funding to train the next generation of STEM workers. Some of the funding provided through the National Defense Education Act and the National Science Foundation focused on training teachers and reworking the high school curriculum. For additional information, see Welch (1979).

characteristics that may help address this problem. First, fifth grade appears to be a particularly appropriate age for a hands-on STEM intervention. Research suggests that students in the fourth to eighth grades have little experience with hands-on curricula, that attitudes formed at these ages are influential in students' future decisions related to STEM course taking and careers, and that low engagement with STEM subjects is especially likely among minority, female, and low-income students (Change the Equation, 2015; U.S. Department of Labor, 2007). Second, unlike many after-school or summer supplemental programs, *all* students in a classroom take part in STARBASE at once rather than only students who have an interest in a subject or who have transportation to attend supplemental programs. Teachers also attend and observe, providing another potential pathway to influence future engagement and achievement. Finally, STARBASE aligns with certain guidelines, such as the design principles established by Change the Equation, to encourage investment in effective programs with the ability to inspire student achievement in STEM subjects (Change the Equation, undated).

Previous research suggests that STARBASE is quite effective on a variety of outcome measures. Considering short-term measures first, students' scores on a test designed to measure comprehension of subjects covered in STARBASE increased substantially after completing the program. Students also indicated higher levels of confidence or efficacy on STEM subjects after attending STARBASE (Wenger, Huff, and Schulte, 2013).

There is also evidence that STARBASE has influence over longer-term outcomes. In particular, a randomized control trial carried out using data from Saint Paul Public Schools in Minnesota indicates that students completing STARBASE had significantly higher levels of interest in technology (and in joining the military) than did similar students who did not complete the program. Test scores and attendance rates both appeared to improve among students who completed STARBASE. High school graduation rates were improved, but only among those who received a higher-than-usual "dose" of the program (by participating in the fourth through sixth grades).[15] In general, participants reported that STARBASE was a positive, formative experience.

Additionally, other analyses comparing various outcomes between those who took part in STARBASE and other similar students suggest that the program has a role in lowering school absences, especially among those who had relatively low scores on standardized tests, and participants had higher scores on statewide standardized

---

[15] These results come from studies focused on separate STARBASE sites and separate outcomes; see Dauphinee et al. (2015), Mohr and Mueller (2012), and Sharpe Solutions (2015). The studies also found differences on other academic outcomes that were generally favorable but not statistically significant (and thus could have occurred by chance). Most students do not have the opportunity to take part in STARBASE across multiple grades, but some students do have the opportunity to participate in the after-school version, STARBASE 2.0. To date there is no existing research on the effectiveness of STARBASE 2.0.

tests, despite the lack of alignment between the test and the STARBASE curriculum (Dauphinee et al., 2015; Sharpe Solutions, 2015).

Yet there is no research on STARBASE's success as an outreach program (or, to our knowledge, on outreach for DoD's other youth programs). With this study, we focus on some new directions for understanding the communities served by STARBASE and the program's potential role in military outreach.

The Organization of This Report

In this chapter we have provided background information on the DoD STARBASE program, including cost trends and the number of participants over time. We have also outlined the purposes of the current study and describe the methodologies used. Finally, we summarized the existing research on STARBASE.

The remainder of this report is organized as follows:

- In Chapter Two we briefly describe our methodology, including our conceptual framework, measures, and data sources.
- In Chapter Three we describe the communities served by STARBASE.
- In Chapter Four we discuss outreach efforts, beginning with direct efforts of individual STARBASE programs and measures related to other less direct pathways of the program's influence, including its institutional presence.
- In Chapter Five we develop and test several potential (but exploratory) measures for the outcomes that could develop as a consequence of the outreach and influence of STARBASE discussed in Chapters Four.
- In Chapter Six we discuss a supplemental analysis that speaks to the possibility of using social media to reach influencers.
- In Chapter Seven we summarize findings and discuss next steps.

CHAPTER TWO

Conceptual Framework, Data Sources, and Measures

In this chapter we describe the data sources and key measures used and conclude with an overview of the outreach model used in this study; this will provide a framework for Chapters Four and Five. Additional information on methodology is provided in Appendix A.

Data Sources

Our analytic data sets comprise a variety of sources of data. To examine the school and neighborhood characteristics of areas with and without STARBASE programs, we compiled a large data set that included a combination of neighborhood, school, and STARBASE administrative data. This data set also included information on military influence and the geographic location of STARBASE and other youth programs, as well as applicants and accessions to the military and community confidence in the military, all of which was used to develop and analyze measures of possible outcomes. Data from these sources were merged together and analyzed at the school district level. This data set is our primary source of data for answering research questions 1 (population served), 3 (indirect program influence), and 4 (possible long-term outcomes).

To answer research question 2 (direct outreach), we compiled data from a survey of STARBASE program directors; we also searched for relevant newspaper stories.[1] Other data sources that supplemented our primary analyses included Google Analytics search data (to learn more about the level of interest in STARBASE), and Joint Advertising Market Research & Studies (JAMRS) data to explore the extent to which social media data is being used by influencers and how websites and social media could potentially be leveraged as greater sources of influence in the future.[2] Influencers are

---

[1] The survey is carried out by DoD and occurs annually; questions include specific inquiries about outreach efforts. Here we used aggregated information from the 2015 survey to quantify directors' outreach efforts.

[2] While the literature on the effectiveness of social media is still in its infancy, there is some evidence that it could be an effective strategy for outreach. Here we use the term *social media* as defined by Kaplan and Haenlein (2010) to include both social networking sites set up to share various information (e.g., Facebook or YouTube), as well as sites focused on searches (e.g., Google). We examine data from Facebook and from Google searches.

adults who are thought to influence students' educational and job choices; examples include parents and grandparents, but also teachers and others who work with young people (see, e.g., Carvalho et al., 2008). Further information on the sources of data and development of our analytic sample is available in Appendix A. Although the data used in this study come from many different sources, we attempt to standardize the time frame throughout our analyses to ensure that our measures were collected as close together as possible. In some cases, this means that we do not use the most recent data available. A summary of data sources is provided in Table 2.1.

Table 2.1
Summary of Data Sources, Measures, and Years

Data Source	Description	Measures	Years Analyzed	Sample	Number of Observations
ACS data	Neighborhood measures	Index of neighborhood disadvantage; % in STEM occupation; % minority; % veteran	Five-year rolling averages for 2009–2013.[*]	All school districts, excluding data from charter and institutional schools and elementary-only districts	13,012
NCES data from CCD	School data	Youth population, Title I students, graduation rates	2011 and 2013	All school districts with fifth grades, excluding data from charter schools	12,745
Uniform Crime Reporting Program data	Crime data	Violent crime rates, property crime rates	2012		12,998
STARBASE administrative data		Start and end year of STARBASE programs; whether there was an active program in 2014	2014	Fifth grade school districts with STARBASE programs	13,595 (250 districts with STARBASE programs)
STARBASE directors' survey	Annual survey of STARBASE directors	Outreach measures used	2015	Survey sent to all STARBASE directors	65
LexisNexis Academic	Search for newspaper articles about STARBASE	Number of newspaper articles	1991–May 2017	LexisNexis database	254
DoD data	Data on applicants and accessions	Applicants, accessions, minorities	FY2011–FY2015		11,143
Google Analytics	Data on relevant searches	Relative number of searches over time	2004–2015	All who used Google to search for relevant terms	N/A
Facebook	Data on activity of STARBASE Facebook accounts	Number of posts, likes; existence of posts other than pictures	Totals as of October 2015	STARBASE Facebook pages	18 STARBASE Facebook pages

Table 2.1—Continued

Data Source	Description	Measures	Years Analyzed	Sample	Number of Observations
JROTC	JROTC program locations	Presence of a JROTC program in district	2015	All programs	3,964
Recruiters	Military recruiter locations	Recruiter influence score	2016	All Army, Air Force, and Navy recruiters	1,315 Army, 699 Air Force, and 793 Navy Recruiters (2,807 total)
Military Influence	Military facility location and population	Presence of a military facility in the district; military influence score (which accounts for the size of the base)	2013–2015	All military facilities; population available for installations with >100 active duty sponsors	425 facilities; 217 installations with population

*Accessed from the U.S. Census Bureau in June 2017.

The analyses addressing research questions 1, 3, and 4 use merged school and neighborhood data analyzed at the school district level. Sample sizes vary slightly for the different analyses due to missing data. For the analyses of neighborhood data, we examined 13,012 school districts, and for analyses using school information, we had a sample of 12,745. There is some additional missing data on crime, leaving us with a sample of 12,988 for the descriptive analyses of crime data. For the final models, we included indicator variables for whether crime data was missing for a district.[3] Finally, for the applicant and accessions analyses, we aggregated to the primary school district level. This reduced our sample to 10,980 school districts with high schools.[4] The points at which we lost data during the matching process is depicted in Figure 2.1.

Measures

Neighborhood Disadvantage

A key step to measuring the outreach of the STARBASE program is to examine the characteristics of the community it serves and whether the program is reaching the intended (disadvantaged) population. To do this, we developed a rich data set that includes many relevant neighborhood and school measures.

---

[3] Because not all counties reported crime statistics, rather than drop all districts with missing data from our final analyses, we include an indicator variable to capture absence in all models, coded 1 if crime data were missing for a school district and 0 otherwise.

[4] Some districts include only elementary schools; in these cases, the schools are also attached to a "primary" school district that includes a high school.

Figure 2.1
Analytic Samples for School, Neighborhood, Crime, and DoD Applicant/Accessions Data

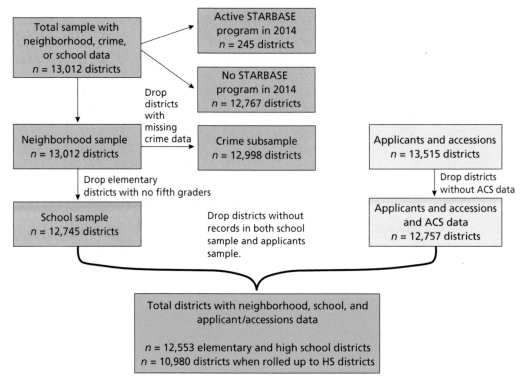

NOTE: This figure demonstrates the formation for our analytic sample from our source data sets. Some districts include only elementary schools, but in these cases the schools are attached to a "primary" district with high schools. Therefore, our sample is smaller (*n* = 10,980) when we analyze districts with high schools. Districts with high schools are relevant when analyzing military applicant/accession data.
RAND *RR2160OSD-2.1*

We were particularly interested in measures that capture the level of disadvantage of neighborhoods, including economic, crime, and other measures of disadvantage. To assess *socioeconomic disadvantage*, we used an index of nine factors, including:

- percentage of residential stability (i.e., percentage of population in the same residence as the previous year)
- percentage receiving public assistance (i.e., percentage of households with public assistance income, including general assistance and Temporary Assistance for Needy Families; this does not include Supplemental Security Income or noncash benefits such as food stamps)
- percentage below the poverty level
- percentage unemployed
- percentage without a vehicle

- percentage with a high school degree
- percentage with a female head of household
- percentage living in overcrowded housing
- median income.

We also examined other measures of *neighborhood context*, including whether neighborhoods include a high proportion of minority residents, the percentage of the population that are veterans, the percentage of foreign born or non–native English speakers, and the level of employment in STEM occupations. Finally, we considered neighborhood crime, adjusted for population.

Direct Outreach

To understand current direct outreach efforts (see Chapter Four), we use the following measures in this report:

- existing relationship-building outreach efforts of STARBASE programs
  - description of the organizations that partner with STARBASE
  - number of organizations that partner with each STARBASE program
- levels of Facebook activity on STARBASE sites
- overall levels of Google search activity related to STARBASE
- variation in Google searches across different geographic regions.

Indirect Influence

To understand how the institutional presence of STARBASE programs might contribute to outreach, we developed a set of measures of military influence. As discussed in Chapter One, the concept of *military institutional presence* was developed by Burk (2001) to explain how the military has maintained a central position as an institution that remains salient, even as it is not present in all communities. Kleykamp (2006) subsequently developed a straightforward and intuitive measure of military presence based on military employment. We expanded upon this notion with several geographic measures of military presence and influence.

Geographic Measure of Youth Program Outreach. We considered the possibility that STARBASE programs may be located in neighborhoods with little other exposure to the military, and thus the program may be particularly crucial for developing feelings of goodwill toward the military. To test this idea, we developed a *geographic measure of military outreach*, which consists of an indication of the presence of a STARBASE or other DoD youth program.

Geographic Measure of Military Presence and Military Influence. To capture a measure of military institutional influence, we constructed two measures from the locations of military bases. Additionally, larger bases are likely to have more impact on the local community than small ones. *Military presence* is a simple construct that captures the presence of a military facility within a school district. Yet, in some cases students may live in a different district from, but quite close to, a military base; we therefore constructed a measure of *military influence* by creating a radius around each military base proportional to its number of active duty servicemembers, with the maximum distance set at 30 miles, as a proxy for the base's impact in the local community and to align with the possible commute distance used in other variables, including recruiter influence. The active duty servicemember population at the largest base, Fort Bragg, was 46,136, where the radius is therefore equal to the maximum of 30 miles. The smallest population was 101, at Naval Support Agency New Orleans, where the radius is therefore 0.066 miles. From there we determined the proportion of each district that lies within the radius of a base. We included all bases with at least 100 persons (thus, we exclude small reserve bases and others that are likely to have minimal influence).

Geographic Measure of Military Recruiters. Our measures of *military influence through access to recruiters* are very similar to our measures of military bases (above), indicating both the presence of a recruiter within the school district and also the proportion within the district living within 30 miles of a recruiter.[5]

Long-Term Outcomes

Although STARBASE is not a recruiting program, creating an interest in and knowledge about the military is part of its mission. Therefore, we examined measures of behaviors and attitudes related to the military. This includes the *number and quality of military applicants and accessions* to determine the extent to which STARBASE programs are located in areas with lower- or higher-than-average levels of military interest (as expressed through applicants and accessions). We also explored public confidence in the military over time and across geography, as recorded in the General Social Survey (GSS).

A Model of DoD's Outreach

We conclude this chapter with a theoretical model of outreach that guides the analyses in Chapters Four and Five. Outreach is a form of communication; indeed, in many cases outreach encompasses several forms of communication. We therefore drew from the communications literature to develop a model of DoD's outreach efforts. This model draws primarily on the work of Larson et al. (2009).[6]

Figure 2.2 shows the flow of DoD's communication efforts; the model as written is specific to STARBASE. Here the model breaks out communication efforts into

---

[5]   We made this selection based on distance rather than travel time, as in some parts of the country travel time differs dramatically with time of day. We tested other, longer distances (60 miles or more), and our results were substantively similar.

[6]   The authors wish to thank Eric Larson for updating his 2009 model for this publication.

Figure 2.2
STARBASE Outreach Efforts

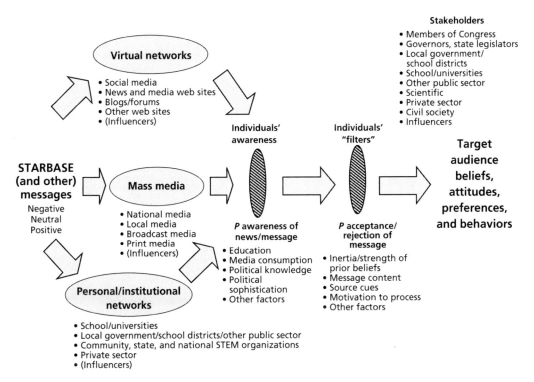

SOURCE: Larson (2017).
NOTE: The model is used to provide a framework for thinking about how outreach efforts operate. Regardless of the number of channels used to communicate, not everyone will become aware of or accepting of the message. The stylized filters express this idea; *P* indicates the probability of awareness and acceptance of the message; the factors below these expressions (e.g., "Education") are potential mediators.
RAND *RR2160OSD-2.2*

those focused on virtual networks (such as social media), those focused on traditional mass media, and those focused on personal or institutional networks. All these channels provide information that flows through filters (because not all information is observed or received at the same rate) to the target audience. The existence of these filters could explain, for example, why some members of a community may have been exposed to outreach efforts but may be unaware of a given program. Here we envision the target audience for outreach as being made up of community members, but the model also explicitly recognizes other stakeholders. Both STARBASE's direct outreach efforts (led by a program director) and its outreach through institutional presence could operate through any of the channels shown in the figure (virtual networks, mass media, personal/institutional networks). And outreach efforts could focus on any or any combination of the stakeholders shown in Figure 2.2. This list of stakeholders provides a reminder that outreach efforts for STARBASE and similar programs could be focused on many different audiences. Existing STARBASE outreach efforts are focused on members of the community; we discuss this in more detail in Chapter Four, and we discuss potential outreach efforts to influencers in Chapter Six.

While the literature on the effectiveness of social media—defined here based on Kaplan and Haenlein (2010) to include both social networking sites set up to share various information (e.g., Facebook or YouTube) and sites focused on searches (e.g., Google)—is still in its infancy, we note that there are suggestions that *converged media* (which could include advertising, websites, and social media) may be an especially effective strategy (see, e.g., Quesenberry, 2016).

Longer-term outcomes of the outreach process are represented at the far right of Figure 2.2 as beliefs, attitudes, preferences, and behaviors. This suggests that many different outcomes could occur in response to DoD's communication efforts, including changes in behaviors, preferences, and attitudes. For example, our model (and the work of Burk, 2001, and Kleykamp, 2006) also suggests that military outreach efforts may be reflected in changing behaviors. One potential measure of these behaviors is the number and/or quality of applicants and/or recruits. Another potential outcome might be positive opinions or attitudes about the military. Especially in the health field, there is evidence that social media strategies can be effective, both as forms of outreach and as levers to change behavior.[7]

While we do not have the type of data that would allow us to measure a *change* in these behaviors and attitudes in response to the establishment of youth programs, we use several data sources (described above) to explore different mechanisms for and potential consequences of STARBASE and related military outreach.

The model in Figure 2.2 also lays out a framework for designing an experiment to test the influence of outreach efforts and for determining causality. We return to this subject in Chapter Seven.

Chapter Summary

In this chapter we began by describing each source of quantitative data used in our analyses. We also provided information on sample sizes and data set construction. Next we described our measures of disadvantage and of outreach/influence. Finally, we presented a model to assist in thinking through the likely outcomes of DoD's outreach efforts. In Chapter Three we compare districts and neighborhoods with STARBASE programs to those without STARBASE programs, thus documenting the extent to which STARBASE programs serve disadvantaged youth.

---

[7]   See, e.g., Korda and Itani (2013). The health field is ahead of other fields in terms of publishing peer-reviewed research on the relationships between social media/internet communications and relevant outcomes. For example, an analysis of Google search data focused on predicting/tracking flu outbreaks (Ginsberg et al., 2009).

CHAPTER THREE

STARBASE Community Characteristics

How Do Community Characteristics Compare in Locations With and Without STARBASE?

We began our analyses by using the rich and varied measures included in the American Community Survey (ACS) to learn more about the neighborhoods that make up school districts with STARBASE programs. We were particularly interested in measures that capture the level of disadvantage of neighborhoods, including socioeconomic, crime, and other measures of disadvantage. These characteristics provide information on the extent to which STARBASE is targeting neighborhoods in the greatest need of STEM outreach. Because we have numerous measures of disadvantage available in the ACS data and they are all highly correlated, we used factor analysis to identify the factors that measure an underlying construct of disadvantage.[1]

Table 3.1 shows the nine factors that make up the resulting *socioeconomic neighborhood disadvantage measure* by whether or not the school district has a STARBASE program. As the table indicates, STARBASE programs do indeed serve schools in disadvantaged neighborhoods. On average, households in school districts with a STARBASE program are less likely to have residential stability, more likely to be receiving public assistance, more likely to be below the poverty level, more likely to have members who are unemployed, less likely to own a vehicle, more likely to be overcrowded, more likely to have a lower median income, and more likely to be a female-headed household than are neighborhoods without a STARBASE program. The only disadvantage that works in the opposite direction is education: households in neighborhoods

---

[1] There is a long history in the social science literature of using confirmatory factor analyses to describe the social and economic characteristics of U.S. geographic areas (typically, census tracts). The general approach is to retain a single factor of disadvantage using some combination of information on such neighborhood measures as level of income, poverty, unemployment, public assistance, female-headed households, educational attainment, and employment in professional or managerial positions. We began with 15 potential measures of disadvantage and, using an exploratory factor analysis approach, identified nine indicators that appeared to fit a single underlying factor structure. The original measures and nine final measures for the disadvantage factors are included in Appendix A, Table A.1.

Table 3.1
Neighborhood Disadvantage Factors in Neighborhoods With and Without the Presence of the STARBASE Program

Measure	STARBASE	No STARBASE
Stability (%)	85.0	87.7
Public assistance (%)	3.3	2.6
Below poverty level (%)	12.0	10.5
Unemployed (%)	5.4	5.0
No vehicle (%)	6.6	5.7
No high school degree (%)	12.3	13.0
Female head of household (%)	6.9	5.8
Crowded housing (%)	3.1	2.5
Median income (mean)	$51,380	$54,317

SOURCE: Authors' calculations, based on analyses of ACS data.

NOTE: n = 13,012 school districts. Due to missing data, for a few measures we have information for only 13,011 districts; for median income we have information for 12,997 districts.

with a STARBASE program are slightly more likely to have a high school degree, on average, although this difference is small.

While each factor shows only a small difference for STARBASE as compared to non-STARBASE neighborhoods, the difference between neighborhoods with and without a STARBASE program is more obvious when we look at the index of disadvantage that includes all the factors, as demonstrated in Figure 3.1, which shows the mean factor score for districts with and without STARBASE programs on a standardized scale, with a mean of 0 and a standard deviation of 1 for the overall sample.[2] The difference in means is statistically significant at p = 0.0003. Appendix A describes the methods used to create the index.

ACS data can also help provide a rich picture of other aspects of the neighborhood context, including whether neighborhoods include a high proportion of minority residents, the percentage of foreign born or non–native English speakers, and the level of employment in STEM occupations. Neighborhoods with these characteristics are prime candidates for STEM outreach. Table 3.2 compares school districts with and without STARBASE programs on a variety of such measures. Relative to districts without STARBASE programs, school districts with STARBASE programs have a larger

---

[2] STARBASE districts have a mean of –0.004; standard deviation is 0.95. Non-STARBASE districts have a mean of 0.22; standard deviation is 1.06.

Figure 3.1
Composite Measure of Neighborhood Disadvantage in Neighborhoods With and Without the Presence of the STARBASE Program

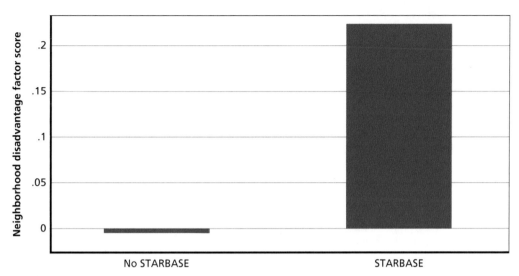

SOURCE: Authors' calculations, based on analysis of ACS data.
NOTE: n = 12,997. Difference is statistically significant at the 1-percent level, indicating that differences are unlikely to have occurred by chance.
RAND RR2160OSD-3.1

Table 3.2
Other Neighborhood Characteristics With and Without the Presence of the STARBASE Program

Measure (%)	STARBASE	No STARBASE
Race/ethnicity: Hispanic	10.6	9.6
Race/ethnicity: black non-Hispanic*	9.1	5.3
Race: Native American or Alaskan Native	1.1	1.2
Foreign-born	6.5	6.0
Non-native English speaker	4.7	4.2
Aged 16+ in military	0.66	0.30
Aged 18+ veteran	10.5	10.1
Aged 16+ in computer science, engineering, or science occupation*	4.2	3.7

SOURCE: Authors' calculations, based on analyses of ACS data.

NOTE: n = 13,012 school districts. Due to missing data, for a few measures we have information for only 13,011 districts.

* Differences are statistically significant at the 1-percent level or better, indicating that the differences are unlikely to have occurred by chance.

percentage of minorities, specifically non-Hispanic blacks (9.1 percent for districts with STARBASE versus 5.3 percent for those without STARBASE). In contrast, districts with STARBASE programs have a slightly—but not statistically significantly—lower percentage of Native American/Alaskan Native students, although the difference is quite small. There are other relevant (though not statistically significant) differences as well. STARBASE school districts have a slightly higher percentage of foreign born and non–native English speakers, as well as Hispanics, and a slightly larger percentage of people aged 16 and over who report being in the military and are veterans. These school districts also have significantly more individuals aged 16 and over who are currently employed in STEM occupations, including computer science, engineering, or science.

Finally, Table 3.3 uses information on published crime rates to examine differences in levels of crime in neighborhoods with and without STARBASE programs. Once again, STARBASE is reaching disadvantaged school districts as measured by crime per 100,000 people. As the table shows, school districts with STARBASE programs had higher property crime rates (2,211 per 100,000 for districts with STARBASE, compared to 258 for those without) and violent crime rates (2,613 for districts with STARBASE, compared to 311 for those without).

We found that while STARBASE programs serve a relatively small proportion of all school districts, they serve relatively large districts: districts with STARBASE make up about 2 percent of all districts, but include about 10 percent of all of the nation's youth under 18. STARBASE is also reaching schools in areas that are most disadvantaged and underrepresented when it comes to STEM knowledge and careers. Districts served by STARBASE have slightly higher proportions of fifth graders who are eligible for free or reduced-price school lunches and of minority students (defined here as black or Hispanic students) than districts that are not served by STARBASE.[3] When we

Table 3.3
Local Crime Rates per 100,000 With and Without the Presence of the STARBASE Program

Measure	STARBASE	No STARBASE
Property crime rate*	2,613	2,211
Violent crime rate*	311	258

NOTE: n = 12,998 school districts with data on crime. Crime data were originally provided at the county level.

*Differences are statistically significant at the 1-percent level or better, indicating that the differences are unlikely to have occurred by chance.

---

[3]   Native American/Alaskan Native students also could be viewed as disadvantaged in terms of educational attainment and STEM exposure (see, e.g., Chang, 2015). Table 3.2 indicates that such populations are roughly evenly distributed between districts with STARBASE programs and those without. These students make up about 1 percent of all students; including them in the Minority youth population in Figure 3.2 does not change the percentage.

Figure 3.2
Percentage of Districts, Students, Disadvantaged Students, and Minority Students with STARBASE Access

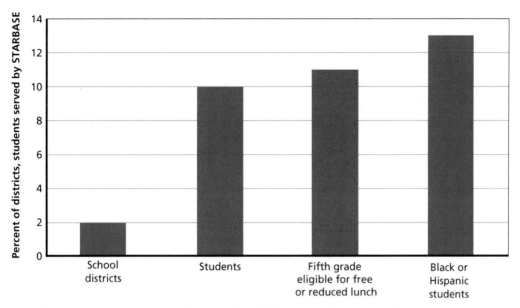

SOURCE: Authors' calculations, based on analysis of NCES, CCD, undated, and ACS data.
NOTE: *n* = 12,721 school districts.
RAND *RR2160OSD-3.2*

include the measure of community disadvantage derived above, we find that nearly one-third of students in districts served by STARBASE are in the most disadvantaged districts.[4] However, districts served by STARBASE actually have *fewer* Native American/Alaskan Native students than districts not served by STARBASE. This may result from the relative distributions of these populations versus military bases (because most STARBASE programs are on military bases). But it suggests that when planning future programs, focusing on serving Native American/Alaskan Native students could be appropriate and could result in an expansion of the relatively disadvantaged populations served by the program.

This discussion of STARBASE neighborhoods and school districts has shown, through a variety of measures, that STARBASE serves a population that is consistent with its intention to focus on serving disadvantaged students. However, positioning the program to reach more Native American/Alaskan Native students would likely be a worthy factor to consider in future location decisions. In the next chapters, we expand our focus to look at a couple of broader measures of outreach.

---

[4] For comparison, one-fourth of all of the nation's students are in the most disadvantaged districts.

Chapter Summary

In this chapter we described the areas that have STARBASE programs; we also compared several measures of neighborhood and school disadvantage for areas with and without STARBASE programs. Our findings indicate the following:

- STARBASE programs serve schools in disadvantaged neighborhoods. On average, households in school districts with a STARBASE program are less likely to have residential stability, more likely to be receiving public assistance, more likely to be below the poverty level, more likely to be unemployed, less likely to own a vehicle, more likely to be overcrowded, more likely to have a lower median income, and more likely to be a female-headed household than are households in neighborhoods without a STARBASE program. We see a statistically significant difference for our overall measure of neighborhood disadvantage, with households in school districts with a STARBASE program being more disadvantaged overall.
- Relative to districts without STARBASE programs, school districts with STARBASE programs have a larger percentage of minorities—especially non-Hispanic blacks.
- School districts with STARBASE programs have higher property crime rates and violent crime rates than districts without the program.
- STARBASE programs are located in relatively large districts, indicating that they have the potential to serve many additional students in Title I schools without expanding into new districts.

CHAPTER FOUR

Direct and Indirect Methods of STARBASE Outreach and Influence

In this chapter we focus first on direct outreach efforts conducted by STARBASE and other youth programs and then turn to indirect pathways of program influence. We begin with a brief description of the relationships that individual STARBASE directors have formed with other local organizations. We then consider the extent to which STARBASE programs use social media as a form of outreach, and the extent to which the public learns about STARBASE through internet searches. Then we turn to the second part of our outreach analysis, which focuses on the ways in which the *presence* of a STARBASE program in a specific city or region might contribute to positive outreach as part of the military's institutional presence. We do this by mapping the locations of DoD's youth programs and assessing their proximity to military bases and recruiters.

Relationships Between STARBASE Programs and Other Local Organizations

STARBASE directors lead outreach efforts for their individual programs, and information about these efforts is available through an annual survey completed by the directors. The survey indicates that the directors focus first on building relationships with local schools and school districts (as these entities choose to send their students to STARBASE). Beyond local elementary schools and districts, programs also build relationships with other organizations in their community—most commonly with local colleges. Nearly two-thirds of directors reported having a relationship with at least one nearby college, but they also reported relationships with other local organizations; indeed, some directors reported relationships with three or more organizations (see Figure 4.1).

STARBASE programs have built relationships with a broad and disparate group of organizations, including Lego robotics programs (which provide opportunities for students to build and design robots for competitions), other STEM-focused programs, Boys and Girls Clubs, museums, chambers of commerce, National Guard Youth ChalleNGe programs, local newspapers, museums, science centers, and local National Guard units.

Figure 4.1
Percentage of STARBASE Programs with Existing Outreach Efforts

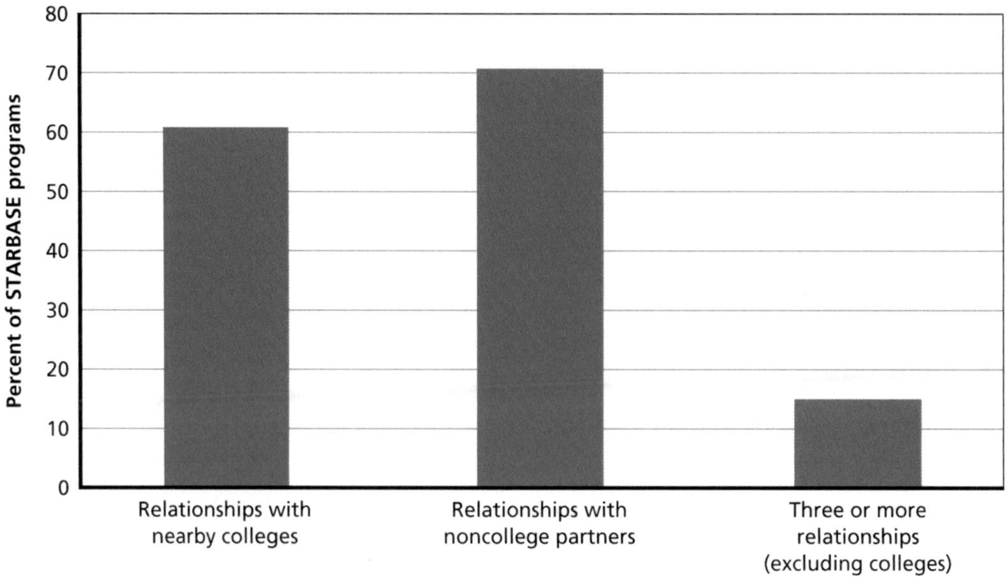

SOURCE: Authors' calculations, based on a 2015 survey of STARBASE directors.
RAND RR2160OSD-4.1

Such relationships can result in additional publicity for the program. For example, we conducted a search for newspaper articles that mention STARBASE, identifying roughly 250 published articles over the period January 1996–July 2017, with most articles published in the last ten years.[1] While relationships between STARBASE and other local organizations can raise awareness of the program, they may be more likely to produce other benefits, such as additions to the curricula, new equipment and supplies, or potential guest speakers for STARBASE events.

Overall, the directors' survey indicates that STARBASE directors have established relationships with a variety of organizations in their local areas. These relationships could form one conduit for STARBASE to create a positive source of outreach for the program and perhaps for DoD more widely.

STARBASE Programs' Use of Social Media

Social media offers another potential method of outreach for programs such as STARBASE, though our analyses indicate, however, that STARBASE programs are not

---

[1]   We used LexisNexis Academic, searched on the word *STARBASE*, and limited the search to newspapers.

Table 4.1
Levels of Activity on STARBASE Facebook Pages

STARBASE Name, Location	Likes	Visitor Posts	Posts Other Than Pictures
Alpena (Michigan)	264	6	No
Austin (Texas)	199	5	**Yes**
Cheyenne (Wyoming)	582	60	No
Ft. Wayne (Indiana)	406	0	No
Houston (Texas)	77	1	No
Indianapolis (Indiana)	140	0	No
Jacksonville (Florida)	197	11	**Yes**
Martinsburg (West Virginia)	1,045	19	No
National	120	0	No
One (Michigan)	341	13	No
Robins (Georgia)	393	33	**No**
Shreveport (Louisiana)	187	1	No
Sioux Falls (South Dakota)	43	0	No
Tulsa (Oklahoma)	32	6	No
West Virginia STARBASE	1,293	100	**Yes**
Wichita (Kansas)	250	14	No
Windsor Locks (Connecticut)	367	23	No
Wright-Patterson Air Force Base (Ohio)	2,333	0	No

NOTE: Authors' tabulations, based on Facebook data, as of October 2015. This table includes all STARBASE Facebook sites that could be located by searching for *STARBASE* on Facebook. During the fall of 2015, there were some 60 STARBASE programs. Thus, most programs appear to have had no Facebook page in the fall of 2015. Some states show up multiple times if there is more than one program in that state.

currently very active on social media. For example, although a number of STARBASE programs have Facebook pages, basic analytics of these pages indicates that overall levels of activity (e.g., visitor posts, comments) are quite low, even though some pages have substantial numbers of "Likes" (see Table 4.1).[2]

---

[2]   We cannot assess how many people visit the Facebook pages for information but do not engage, so these numbers could underestimate impact.

Consistent with these findings, Google Trends data indicate that overall levels of search activity related to STARBASE are quite low.[3] On the whole, STARBASE outreach efforts tend to be very local in nature and focused on relationship building, and do not make much use of social media. Given that the program is targeted to fifth graders, this appears appropriate, and encouraging sites to make additional social media efforts does not seem likely to pay significant dividends. It therefore might make sense to focus *some* STARBASE outreach on social media platforms—not at the level of each individual program, but more broadly. One option would be to focus resources on providing information about STARBASE to the general public, as part of a much broader outreach effort to increase awareness and positive impressions among influencers. We discuss this option further in Chapter Six.

Indirect Outreach: Where Are STARBASE and Other Youth Programs Located?

As discussed above, outreach can occur through the direct efforts of program directors or it can occur via indirect influence that comes from program presence. The rest of this chapter focuses on the geographic location of youth programs and the role program placement could play in influence and outreach. Figures plot the locations of DoD's youth outreach programs (by the school district in which the program is located). Figure 4.2 shows locations of STARBASE programs, Figure 4.3 plots National Guard Youth ChalleNGe programs, and Figure 4.4 plots JROTC programs.[4] Perusing the maps suggests that there is significant overlap among programs in some regions; some locations have one or two types of military programs, while others have no programs.

We compared the locations of these youth programs to each other and to the locations of military recruiters. Among these programs, JROTC, unsurprisingly, has by far the largest number of locations: more than 1,600 school districts have at least one JROTC program. ChalleNGe and STARBASE are, of course, much smaller in scope. But a simple analysis of the overlap indicates that nearly one-third of ChalleNGe programs, and the majority of STARBASE programs, are located in districts that do not

---

[3]   Some of the Google Trends results reported here are likely to overestimate the true number of relevant STARBASE searches; analyses of related searches suggested that some who search for the term *STARBASE* are in fact searching for *Star Trek STARBASE*. Google AdWords does provide the capacity to determine the total number of searches; a drawback of these data is that they are available only for a two-year window. But our analyses of these data indicated that for the years 2013–2015, *STARBASE DoD* was searched about 110 times per month (across the United States) while *STARBASE program* was searched about 50 times per month. These are very low numbers; the term *Army* is searched some 1.5 million times per month.

[4]   In Figure 4.3, we indicate the physical location of each ChalleNGe program. Note, however, that ChalleNGe programs attract youth from across the state in which they are located. ChalleNGe participants perform hundreds of thousands of hours of community service per year (Wenger et al., 2017), and this service generally is performed near the location of the program. Thus, while ChalleNGe may serve as a form of outreach throughout the state, we postulate that the effect will be stronger near the program location, as indicated in Figure 4.2.

Figure 4.2
School Districts with STARBASE Programs, 2014

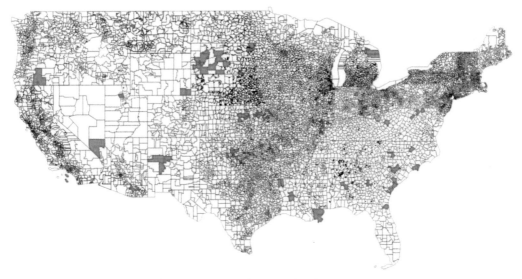

SOURCE: Authors' tabulations, from STARBASE administrative data.
NOTE: Figure indicates the districts in which STARBASE programs are located, but programs are open to students statewide.
RAND *RR2160OSD-4.2*

Figure 4.3
School Districts with National Guard Youth ChalleNGe Programs, 2014

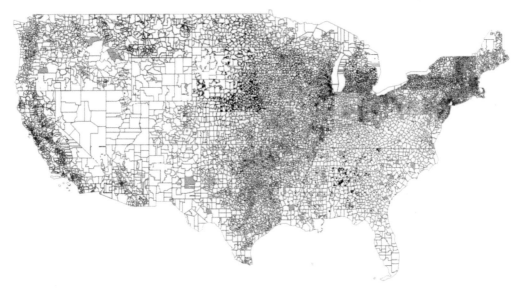

SOURCE: Authors' tabulations, from National Guard Youth ChalleNGe administrative data.
RAND *RR2160OSD-4.3*

Figure 4.4
School Districts with JROTC Programs, 2014

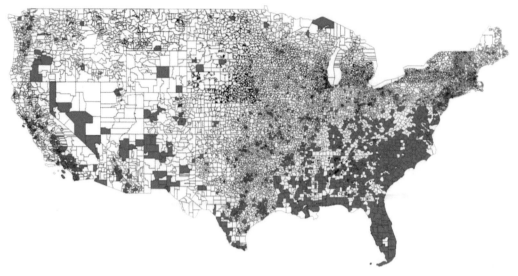

SOURCE: Authors' tabulations, from JROTC administrative data.
RAND RR2160OSD-4.4

have any other DoD youth program. While some areas may have exposure to the military through other means (e.g., military bases), this suggests that ChalleNGe and STARBASE serve to expand the footprint of DoD's youth programs and thus could serve an important outreach function. For example, we might expect that the presence of these programs could influence the population by changing attitudes, and perhaps even propensity, toward military service. We used all these data on STARBASE and other youth program locations to inform subsequent analyses.

Chapter Summary

Our analyses of STARBASE's direct outreach efforts, including local relationship building and social media use, resulted in the following finding:

- To date, STARBASE programs' outreach efforts are largely local and do not utilize social media; rather, outreach efforts consist primarily of specific relationships between individual STARBASE programs and relevant local organizations. While a national outreach strategy could include aspects of social media, our findings suggest that people do not currently actively use this form of media.

Our analyses of STARBASE's indirect influence, captured by youth program and other military geographic presence, resulted in the following findings:

- While there is significant overlap in the locations of youth programs, some regions have more than one youth program, while others have none.
- JROTC, unsurprisingly, has by far the largest number of locations; however, nearly one-third of ChalleNGe programs, and the majority of STARBASE programs, are located in districts with no other youth program outreach efforts.

CHAPTER FIVE

Possible Long-Term Outcomes

Our outreach model in Chapter Two suggested that youth programs could serve as a mechanism to influence various longer-term outcomes, such as attitudes toward the military or propensity toward military service. In this chapter we explore measures that could capture the longer-term success of military outreach efforts such as the STARBASE program: the number and quality of military applicants and accessions, and public attitudes toward the military. We use these measures to demonstrate some types of outreach measures that could be developed to capture the longer-term impact of outreach efforts.

We caution that these outcome measures and analyses should be seen as exploratory. We recognize explicitly that our results are not causal in nature; even in cases when military presence and/or youth programs are correlated with applicants or accessions, the presence of military personnel or youth programs might not have *caused* a change in the number of applicants or accessions. Determining causality would require a different analytic approach, such as measuring the number of applicants or accessions before and after a change in the military presence, or through the use of a truly experimental design, both of which are beyond the scope of this study.

Below we highlight the key findings, first for our analysis of the applicant and accessions data and then for attitudinal data or self-reported confidence in the military. More detailed output from our models is available in Appendix B. We return to a discussion of possible next steps for capturing and analyzing outcomes of outreach in Chapter Seven.

Number and Quality of Applicants and Accessions

The number and quality of applicants and accessions are measures that could reflect positive military influence. If individuals live in areas with high levels of military influence (as measured by the location of military bases and recruiters), they might be more aware of military opportunities and thus more likely to apply for military positions and/or access.

We examined the following outcomes to capture the number of enlisted applicants and accessions:

- The number of applicants and accessions per population based on data from the U.S. Military Entrance Processing Command, averaged across fiscal years 2011–2015.
- The percentage of accessions that meet the *high-quality standard*, defined as accessions with a score at or above the fiftieth percentile on the Armed Forces Qualification Test *and* a high school diploma or equivalent credential.

We began by carrying out a series of specification tests to choose the most appropriate measures for the regression model; we excluded variables that were highly correlated with other variables in the model (for example, the percentage of the population that spoke a language other than English at home was highly correlated with the percentage of the population that was foreign born; we included only the indicator for foreign born). Our final model included the following measures: neighborhood disadvantage (scale), the violent crime rate, the property crime rate, an indicator that the dropout rate is in the top quartile, the percentage of black and Hispanic residents in a neighborhood, a recruiter influence score, military presence in the district, the percentage of people who are foreign born, the percentage of people who are servicemembers, the percentage of people who are veterans, the percentage of fifth graders who are in Title I schools, whether the district has a youth program, and an indicator of the census division.[1] We examined results separately for urban, suburban, and rural school districts. To examine the relationship between our applicant and accession outcomes and school- and neighborhood-level predictors, we ran a series of linear regression models. Complete regression results are included in Appendix B.

The results generally suggest that there are more applicants and accessions in areas where a higher proportion of the population is or has been associated with the military. This is consistent with earlier findings. We found that *military presence* (which denotes a military base in the school district) and *recruiter influence* (which denotes the presence of a recruiter within 30 miles) were positively correlated with the outcomes of interest in several cases. In addition, both the percentage of servicemembers and the percentage of veterans in the local area were positively correlated with most of our outcomes of interest.

Holding constant the measures of military presence, we found that, in urban and suburban areas, having a youth program in the district is associated with more (enlisted) applicants, and that districts in suburban areas have more accessions if they have a youth program (see Figure 5.1). While these results do not establish causality,

---

[1]   U.S. states are divided into the following census divisions: New England, Middle Atlantic, South Atlantic, East South Central, West South Central, East North Central, West North Central, Mountain, and Pacific. For more information and a list of the states in each division, see U.S. Census Bureau, geography landing page, n.d.

Figure 5.1
Applicants and Accessions in Areas with Youth Programs

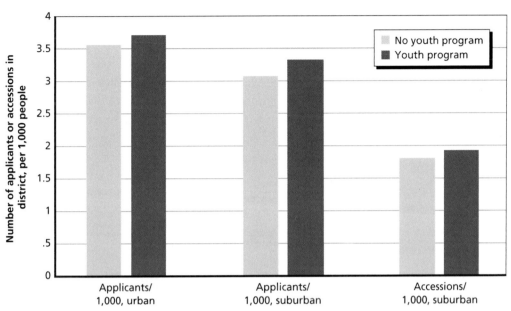

SOURCE: Authors' tabulations, based on analyses of ACS data.
NOTE: *n* = 13,011 school districts. Displayed here are the model-predicted numbers of applicants and accessions per 1,000 holding all other model covariates at their mean values.
RAND *RR2160OSD-5.1*

this is consistent with youth programs creating more positive impressions of the military. The results indicate that the number of applicants is about 4 percent higher in urban areas that have a youth program versus those that do not, and that the number of applicants in suburban areas that have youth programs is nearly 8 percent higher than the number in suburban areas that do not. The difference in accessions is roughly the same size in suburban areas; there is no correlation between applicants and youth programs in rural areas, or between accessions and youth programs in urban or rural areas. Finally, there is no correlation between the presence of youth programs and the proportion of applicants who meet the *high-quality standard*.

Next we explore another potential measure of military influence: the public's confidence in the military.

Public Attitudes Toward the Military

In addition to *behaviors* that could be linked to military influence (e.g., applicants and accessions), we also consider *attitudes* toward the military as a potential measure. We used data from the GSS to explore public attitudes toward the military over time and across geography. Since the early 1970s, the GSS has sampled a random subset of the population every year to monitor societal change and attitudes. One question of relevance for this analysis asks about confidence in a range of institutions, including the military. As Figure 5.2 shows, confidence in the military has been on the rise over time, in contrast to confidence in the Executive Branch, confidence in Congress, or confidence in the Supreme Court, all of which have shown moderate declines in recent years and are quite low compared to levels recorded over much of the previous four decades. Figure 5.2 also shows variation over time in public confidence in the military, with upticks in the early 1990s and the first ten years of the twenty-first century. Although it is not shown in Figure 5.2, confidence in other institutions, such as religious, education, medical, and scientific institutions, changed much less over this time period.

Given the variation in military presence and other neighborhood characteristics among locations with STARBASE and other youth programs, we expected to see variation in the levels of military confidence as well. Restricted GSS data are available with geographic indicators and can be linked at the state level to examine variation in rela-

Figure 5.2
Americans' Confidence in Institutions

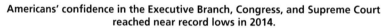

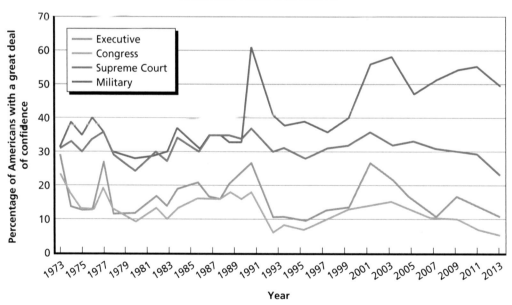

Question: I am going to name some institutions in this country. As far as the people running these institutions are concerned, would you say you have a great deal of confidence, only some confidence, or hardly any confidence at all in them? [Executive Branch/Congress/Supreme Court/Military]

SOURCE: Associated Press–NORC Center for Public Affairs Research, undated (calculated from GSS data).
RAND RR2160OSD-5.2

Figure 5.3
DoD Youth Programs and Military Confidence

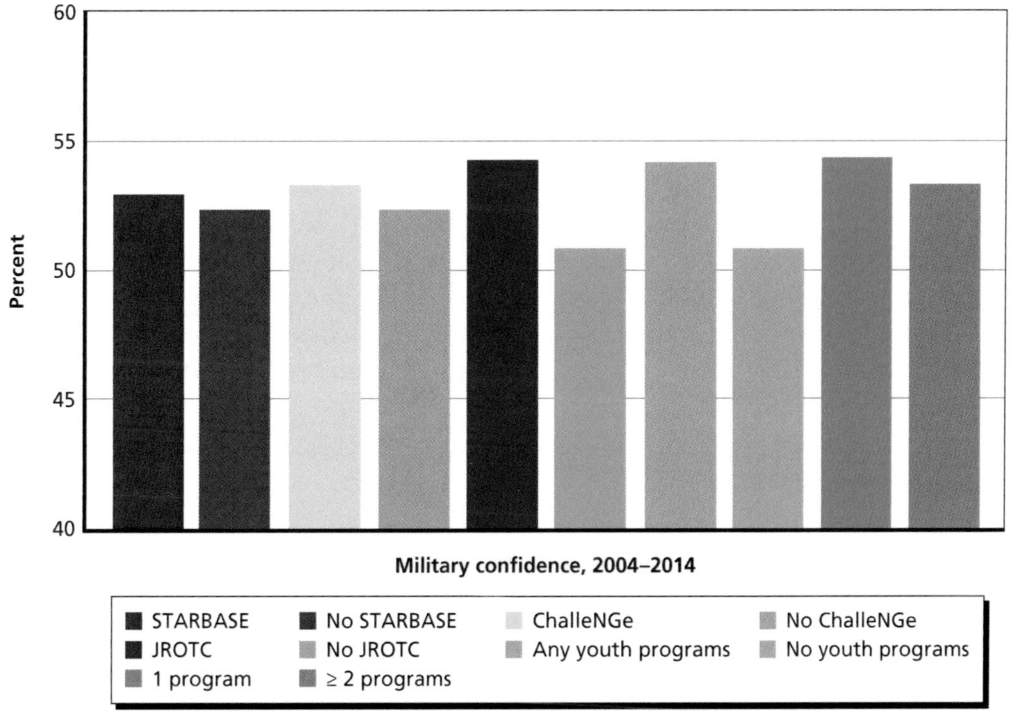

SOURCE: Authors' tabulations, based on GSS data. All differences are statistically significant at the 5-percent level or better, indicating that the results are unlikely to have occurred by chance.
RAND RR2160OSD-5.3

tion to other contextual factors.[2] We used data from the years 2004–2014 on military confidence to create a measure of confidence; our measure indicates the percentage of respondents who expressed a great deal of confidence in the military.

In general, data from the GSS indicate that youth programs are located in districts with relatively high state-level measures of military confidence (see Figure 5.3). However, the difference in military confidence between districts with STARBASE or ChalleNGe programs and those without is markedly smaller than the difference in districts with and without JROTC programs. That is, the STARBASE and ChalleNGe programs appear to be located in states with somewhat lower levels of military confidence than states with JROTC programs. As described earlier in this chapter, STARBASE and ChalleNGe are frequently located in areas with no JROTC program;

---

[2] While indicators are available from the GSS for smaller geographic regions (e.g., census block and county level), the sample sizes are small. Thus, for this analysis, we focused on state-level variation. Indeed, even when we combined data across the years 2004–2014, a few of the smallest states had no observations.

in this sense, they serve to increase the footprint of DoD's youth programs beyond that associated with JROTC programs. We see very little difference in areas with one program compared to those with more than one program, which suggests that in terms of this measure of military confidence there is little additional gain from having exposure to more than one program.

Although they are not shown in the Figure 5.3, there were some unexpected patterns related to areas with higher and lower levels of military confidence. For example, military confidence was positively correlated with military presence but negatively correlated with the percentage of the population who are veterans. We also tested military confidence as an outcome measure in specifications similar to our models of applicants and accessions discussed above, finding that military confidence is negatively correlated with the presence of youth programs (after holding constant all of the other factors in our model). To some extent, these results could be driven by the aggregated nature of military confidence, which is measured at the state level. We do not interpret this result as causal; rather, we interpret it to mean that, after correcting for other factors that are related to military confidence, youth programs appear to be located in areas with lower-than-expected levels of military confidence. To the extent that the programs serve to increase military confidence, this likely represents desirable placement. Having a better understanding of the factors that shape military confidence, and the changes in this measure over time, would be helpful in determining the extent to which measures of military confidence can indicate the success of military outreach efforts.

Chapter Summary

In this chapter we examined exploratory data on how locations with STARBASE programs differ on key outcomes related to military influence. We found the following:

- Holding constant the measures of military presence, having a youth program in the district (in urban and suburban areas) was associated with more (enlisted) military applicants, and districts in suburban areas with youth programs have more accessions.
- Analysis of data from the GSS show that confidence in the military has been on the rise in the United States compared to confidence in other government institutions.
- In general, DoD youth programs are located in districts with relatively high state-level measures of military confidence, although STARBASE and ChalleNGe programs appear to be located in areas with somewhat lower levels of military confidence than are JROTC programs (as measured at the state level).

CHAPTER SIX

The Potential to Expand Outreach to Influencers Through Social Media

In Chapter Four we documented the outreach efforts of individual STARBASE programs, and also explored the role of internet searches as an outreach tool. We found that most STARBASE programs' outreach efforts are local in nature, and that this is likely a preferred strategy, as fifth graders and their parents appear to learn about STARBASE (and about comparable programs) through means other than basic internet searches. But fifth grade students and their parents are not the only audience of DoD's youth outreach efforts. Because we are interested in potential options for expanding outreach related to STARBASE and DoD's other youth programs, in this chapter we consider what is known about a key outreach group—influencers—and their interactions with social media and with other sources of information about DoD.

Most young people make decisions regarding military service in consultation with adults, and thus the role of these adults is viewed as key to the decisionmaking process.[1] Parents, grandparents, and other adults who are likely to influence the decisions of young people are referred to as *influencers*. Although youth programs are not recruiting programs, they may still have a positive effect on influencers, and thus affect the military decisions of youth. Therefore, an understanding of how influencers engage with media sources and obtain information about DoD's programs can help inform STARBASE and other youth programs' outreach efforts.

To address the question of how influencers use websites and social media to gain information about the military, we used data from JAMRS, a DoD program that, among other things, examines the perceptions, beliefs, and attitudes American youth and influencers have about the military. The JAMRS Influencer Poll, which has been conducted quarterly by telephone since 2003, is a companion to the long-running JAMRS Futures Poll for measuring youth attitudes about military service; its specific focus is "to measure an influencer's likelihood to recommend military

---

[1] See, e.g., Orvis et al., 2016. In earlier work, Legree et al. (2000) examined cases in which parental and child attitudes differed, and found that parental attitudes were also influential in these cases.

service to youth and to support a youth's decision to join the Military" (Carvalho et al., 2008, p. 1).[2] JAMRS asked influencers about their attitudes toward youth joining the military, toward the military more generally, and on a variety of other topical modules.

Unless otherwise noted, analyses in this chapter focus on a wave of the Influencer Poll collected in the spring of 2013 that included an additional battery of questions related to influencer use of social media.[3] These questions focused on the type and frequency of social media generally used, as well as specific contact with military websites and social media accounts. We used these data to understand how social media and other media inform influencer impressions of the military, which influencers report engagement with DoD-based websites, and how they differ from influencers who do not have such engagement.

Which Media Are Shaping Influencers' Impressions of the Military?

Social media is just one of many media sources that influencers draw information from in forming their impressions of the military. We compared the role of social media to that of other media sources in shaping influencers' impressions of the military, and also assessed the net positivity of those impressions, as well as influencer perceptions of the trustworthiness of that source.

Figure 6.1 shows influencers' reported sources of their impressions of the military. The area of each circle indicates the extent to which influencers reported that the source influenced their impressions of the military: the larger the circle, the greater number of respondents who said they were influenced by the source. Thus, "Television" (TV) and "Things you've read" (TR) are the two most influential sources of information; "Social media" (SM) is considered a less influential source of military information.[4] The location of the circle on the vertical axis indicates the perceived trustworthiness of the source; while "Things you've read" and "Radio" are considered more trustworthy

---

[2]   In the case of this poll, JAMRS defines *influencers* as parents, grandparents, and other adults who report influencing youth ages 12–24. (Other adults include teachers, coaches, religious leaders, mentors, relatives, and any other individuals who interact closely with youth.) The JAMRS survey uses this precise definition to screen and identify influencers among survey participants; we use the same language to refer to the same group. See Appendix C for more information on our analyses of the JAMRS Influencer Poll data.

[3]   Data from the 2013 wave of the Influencer Poll were used, as this wave had the largest sample of respondents and the broadest range of questions included. The findings from all analyses were confirmed to the best degree possible based on available variables in the 2014 and 2015 waves of the Influencer Poll.

[4]   It is possible that respondents include some things that they read online when considering the body of "Things you've read."

Figure 6.1
Positive Impressions, Trust, and Usage Levels of Media Sources

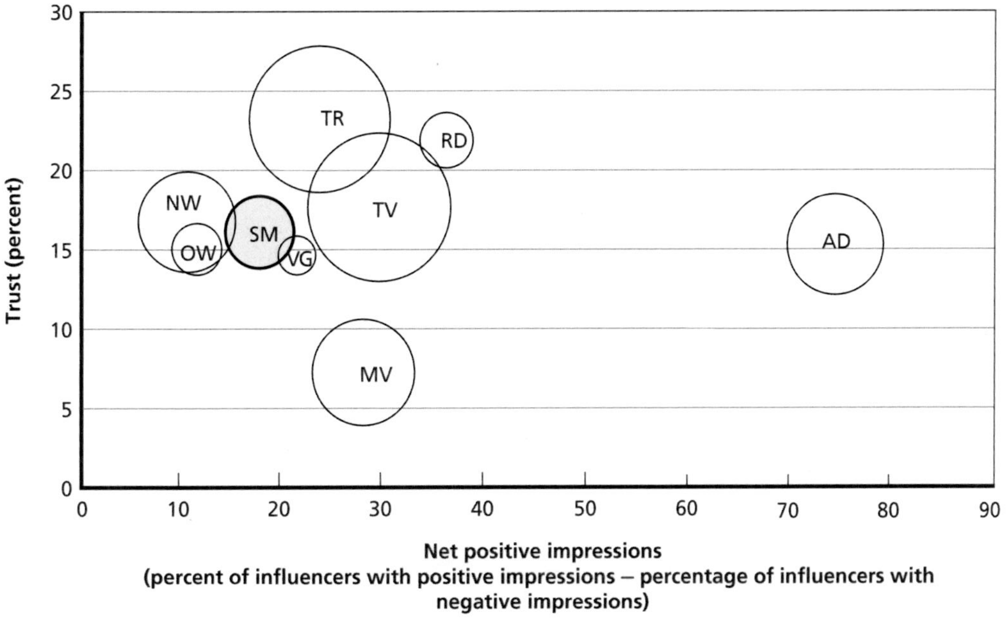

SOURCE: JAMRS Influencer Poll, 2013.
NOTE: n = 1,188. The relative usage level of each media source is indicated by the area of the circle.
AD = Advertisements; MV = Movies; NW = News website; OW = Other website; RD = Radio; SM = Social
media; TR = Things you've read; TV = Television; VG = Video games.
RAND RR2160OSD-6.1

than other sources, "Social media" is considered roughly as trustworthy as most other
sources.[5] See Appendix C for additional information.

Finally, respondents were asked to indicate how positive their impressions of the
military were by source; the horizontal axis indicates the net percentage of impressions
from each source that were considered positive. In this case, impressions from social
media were less positive than impressions from many other sources; the exceptions
were news websites and other websites. Note that sources of positive impressions were
not always viewed as trustworthy. It is unsurprising that advertisements provided the
most positive impressions; this it to be expected, as advertisements are the one area in

---

[5]   Consistent with other JAMRS presentations of these data, we calculate positive impressions as the percentage of respondents indicating that a source gave them "Mostly positive" or "Completely positive" impressions
of the military. Negative impressions are calculated the same for "Completely negative" and "Mostly negative"
responses. Net positive impressions are defined by subtracting the negative impressions from the positive impressions. Trustworthiness is defined as the percentage of respondents who indicated that they trusted the source "A
lot" or "Completely." See Appendix C, and especially table C.1, for more information about the JAMRS data and
media impressions.

which DoD entirely controls the message, leading to more positive content. But this source was viewed as somewhat less trustworthy than other generally positive sources like television or radio. In contrast, trust was highest in "Things you've read," although levels of trust were fairly low for all sources. Websites—both news sites and others— were viewed least positively.[6]

In general, social media was grouped largely with the other new media sources (including news websites, other websites, and video games) in terms of positive or negative impressions and trust. These sources give less positive impressions than television, but have similar levels of trust. Influencers reported using new media sources less than traditional media, including advertisements, television, movies, and things they had read. Only about 10 percent of influencers reported that social media influenced their impressions of the military.

To summarize, some respondents to the JAMRS Influencer Poll indicated that social media was a source of information on the military, and social media is similar to other sources in terms of trustworthiness and net positive impressions.

We also examined trends in the frequencies of various media being reported by influencers. Between 2013 and 2015, the proportion of influencers who reported gaining impressions from social media increased from 10 percent to 16 percent, while the number of people who reported gaining impressions from other sources remained essentially unchanged.[7] Thus, a key finding of our analyses is that social media is the only type of media that is growing as a source of impressions among influencers. A social media–based outreach strategy could capitalize on this growth, especially if the trend continues. Indeed, this growth positions social media as a key outreach avenue for future DoD programs. Taken together, these findings suggest that social media could form a key aspect of DoD's outreach strategy, especially if the cost of impressions created via social media is relatively low.

We also disaggregated the use of social media platforms by age, veteran status, and gender; the results are shown in Figure 6.2.[8] Younger influencers, defined as those under 45 years of age, reported using social media more than older influencers and receiving more positive impressions of the military, although this difference was not statistically significant.[9] Veteran influencers were significantly less likely to say that media sources impacted their impression of the military, as one would expect given

---

[6]   These sources left positive impressions with roughly 33 percent of respondents and negative impressions with roughly 22–23 percent of respondents, yielding about 10 percent net positive impressions.

[7]   Recall that we primarily utilized the 2013 poll, as the sample was larger and the list of questions was more complete; here we compare responses to a single question included in the 2013, 2014, and 2015 polls. Further detail is available in Appendix C, and especially figure C.1.

[8]   See Perrin (2015). We also examined the data by subgroup; influencers reported very similar sources of media impressions regardless of race/ethnicity, education, or income.

[9]   The reason for the relatively high threshold for classifying influencers as younger is that the sample includes only influencers who tend to be somewhat older than the population as a whole. Other sources tend to find greater differences in social media use between, for example, twenty-somethings and forty-somethings; see Perrin (2015).

Figure 6.2
Social Media Platform Use by Age

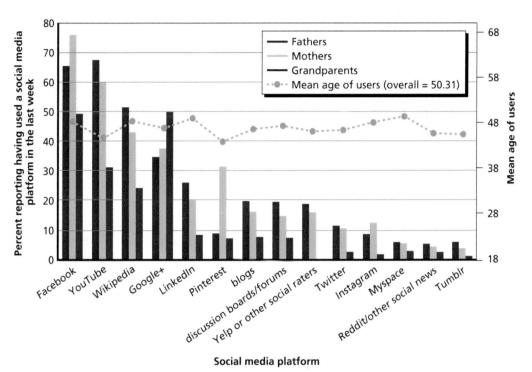

SOURCE: JAMRS Influencer Poll, 2013.
NOTE: *n* = 1,188.
RAND *RR2160OSD-6.2*

their own firsthand experience with it. Female influencers were significantly more likely than male influencers to say that social media influenced their impression of the military.[10] Thus, social media efforts may be more likely to reach some influencers and may create less of an impression on others—although, given rapid changes in the use of these approaches, use of social media will likely continue to evolve. Periodically tracking these trends through the JAMRS polls and other sources will be necessary to ensure that outreach strategies remain relevant.

Which Influencers Engage with Online DoD Content?

The JAMRS Influencer Poll also provides information about the extent to which respondents already engage with DoD online content. Specifically, the poll asks whether respondents have ever looked for information on a military website or a military social media account and also asks influencers to rate their likelihood of

---

[10] Of influencers who indicated social media informed their impression of the military, 65 percent were women, compared to 55 percent of the overall sample (*p* = 0.02).

recommending military service and their self-reported level of knowledge about the military. Each of these variables, along with age, veteran status, and other characteristics, might be associated with a level of engagement with DoD content. We use regression analyses to untangle the correlations between these characteristics.[11]

The results indicate that influencers who engage with DoD's content online tend to be more willing to recommend military services and have higher levels of military knowledge than those who do not. The results also indicate, not surprisingly, that those who use social media more frequently are more likely to engage with DoD's online content. Age, perhaps for the reasons described earlier, does not have a clear relationship with these outcomes, although age is related to the type of platform used within social media. Veteran status and being younger than 45 years of age were also associated with a higher probability of visiting a military website, but these differences were not statistically significant for DoD's social media sites.

These results suggest that DoD's social media campaigns are most likely to reach engaged influencers who are already quite likely to recommend military service. The implication is that other sources (e.g., more general media campaigns focused on non-DoD sites) may be needed to reach influencers who are not predisposed to recommend military service. On the other hand, these results suggest that there is an engaged audience of influencers who visit DoD's platforms regularly and are likely to absorb information presented on these platforms.

Chapter Summary

Influencers are considered a key group in DoD's outreach efforts because of their role in providing information and opinions to young people considering military service (and, presumably, to others in their communities). The JAMRS Influencer Polls provide specific information about how influencers interact with social media in general, and with DoD's websites and social media accounts in particular.

Our analyses of JAMRS data found the following:

- Influencers engaging with online DoD content tend to be comfortable with the DoD and military service (i.e., they are more willing to recommend military service and report higher levels of knowledge of the military than other influencers). Given the limited temporal nature of our data we cannot determine whether this is a result of social media engagement or if this attitude existed prior to any social media engagement.

---

[11] We used logistic regressions, with either engaging with DoD websites or DoD social media platforms as the dependent variable; we included measures of age, gender, influencer type, race/ethnicity, census region of residence, education, income, prior military service, frequency of social media usage, willingness to recommend military service, and knowledge of the military as predictors. All models utilized the weights provided with the survey. See Appendix C for more details; regression results appear in tables C.2 and C.3.

- While social media is not currently a major source of influencer impressions of the military, it is expanding as a source of information faster than any other type of media, suggesting that, despite its relatively minor role as a source of impressions among influencers, it could become an increasingly valuable avenue of future outreach efforts, especially as the cohort of influences change with time to represent individuals who grew up with social media.
- In terms of the quality of the impressions created (i.e., as measured by trust and positivity of impressions), social media is viewed by influencers in a similar manner to how traditional media sources are viewed. These results suggest that an outreach strategy based on social media may be at least as effective as those based on other media.

One interpretation of these results is that DoD's current outreach efforts are most likely to reach those influencers who are already inclined to recommend military service, as these influencers appear more likely than others to engage with DoD's outreach efforts. This suggests that STARBASE (and other youth programs) could have an important role in reaching influencers who are not already engaged with DoD's efforts, and perhaps even influencers who are not inclined to recommend military service. It also suggests that STARBASE's outreach efforts may be more effective if they operate outside the realm of DoD's other existing efforts. To some extent, STARBASE already does this, as each local program establishes relationships with local partners and produces stories in local newspapers. This suggests that especially in the case of programs located in areas with lower levels of confidence in the military as an institution, STARBASE youth programs could serve a valuable outreach function.

CHAPTER SEVEN

Concluding Thoughts and Recommendations

DoD's STARBASE program serves fifth graders from disadvantaged school districts, providing hands-on activities as part of an innovative curriculum focused on STEM. The primary purpose of STARBASE is to increase students' interest in STEM subjects, and evidence from earlier studies indicates that the program accomplishes this purpose. But like DoD's other youth programs, STARBASE is designed as an outreach program with the additional goal of creating positive bonds and engagement between communities and the military. In this report we have described the characteristics of communities reached by STARBASE, the direct outreach efforts of individual STARBASE programs, and the indirect influence that could occur through program placement; we have considered the implications of STARBASE's outreach mission, and have begun to develop exploratory long-term outreach measures for STARBASE and DoD's other youth outreach programs.

Key Findings

Key findings from our research include the following:

- Our first research question asked whether STARBASE is reaching the disadvantaged populations it is designed to reach. There is strong evidence that STARBASE serves a relatively disadvantaged population, as the program intends. For example, school districts with STARBASE programs serve a disproportionately high proportion of children from poor homes, and a disproportionately high proportion of minority youth. The exception to this statement is that Native American/Alaskan Native students are less likely to be present in districts served by STARBASE. This suggests that considering the locations of these populations during any future expansion of STARBASE could result in the program reaching a wider range of disadvantaged youth.
- Our next research question focused on the direct outreach efforts employed by STARBASE program directors. To date, STARBASE programs' outreach efforts

are largely local and consist primarily of specific relationships between individual STARBASE programs and relevant local organizations. While we have no measure of the effectiveness of these efforts, they have the potential to improve community relations and public perceptions of the military. Current efforts appear not to make much use of social media.

- Our research also indicates that social media campaigns sponsored by DoD (through a DoD website, for example) are likely to reach an audience that is already comfortable with DoD and military service. While social media is not currently a major source of influencer impressions of the military, existing data suggest that social media is viewed as a relatively trustworthy source of information, and one that is likely to become increasingly relevant in the future based on current trends.
- We also examined indirect outreach that could occur through program placement. DoD's STARBASE and ChalleNGe programs may be especially well situated to create positive outreach. Across the board we found that youth programs are located in areas with relatively high levels of trust in the military, but in the cases of STARBASE and ChalleNGe, the difference in trust between areas with and without such programs is very small, suggesting that some of the programs are located in areas with lower levels of trust in the military.
- Our final research question focused on potential measures that could capture the impact of outreach. There are many *potential* measures of outreach (although virtually no established measures). We developed simple models of the number of military applicants, the number of military accessions, and the quality of military accessions, and included a variety of local factors that would likely be correlated with applicants and accessions, as well as indicators of DoD youth programs and of military presence. Our results indicate that districts with youth programs have more military applicants than would be expected, even after correcting for a variety of other factors. The results also indicate that the presence of a military base is correlated with applicants and accessions in some areas.

Recommendations and Next Steps

Based on the findings of this research, we make the following recommendations for next steps:

Explore the use of increased social media outreach for DoD youth programs. STARBASE programs' outreach efforts are focused on building relationships with local organizations. This appears to be completely appropriate. However, social media is growing as a source of influencer impressions of the military, while more traditional media sources have seen no growth. In addition, our analysis shows that currently only about 10 percent of influencers reported that social media influenced their impressions of the military. This suggests that there is room to enhance the influence of social media and better use this tool to improve perceptions of STARBASE and the DoD more generally. A social media campaign focused on influencers has the potential to increase knowledge of and support for STARBASE. Another option is a campaign that focuses on retaining interest in STEM subjects and seeks to maintain a connection with those who participate in STARBASE. Such a campaign could also involve DoD's other youth programs and be run centrally (rather than allocating responsibility to individual programs). Measuring the effectiveness of such a campaign would require collecting data on public/influencer perceptions of the military at a fairly local level, both before and after the campaign.

Centrally manage DoD's youth programs to maximize impact. Measuring outreach efforts poses a substantial challenge. Our results represent a first step in measuring the extent to which DoD's youth programs are providing outreach. However, more work is necessary to develop and test appropriate measures of outreach and the long-term impact of outreach efforts. There are many advantages to managing programs together. One advantage identified in this report is that if the youth programs are considered as a group, placement decisions could be made to maximize both access to the programs and potential outreach. In general, our results suggest that placing youth programs in areas away from other outreach efforts could yield positive results.

Work toward a better understanding of the relationships between youth programs, military institutional presence, and the public's perceptions of DoD. Establishing improved measures of outreach would assist DoD in measuring the extent to which youth programs achieve this aspect of their missions. As we have shown in this report, youth programs often are located in areas with few other sources of military influence. While our results are exploratory and not causal, they do indicate that there are more applicants, and sometimes more accessions, in areas with youth programs. In addition, existing STARBASE and ChalleNGe programs appear to be placed in states with lower levels of military confidence than are JROTC programs. Together these results suggest that tracking confidence at a finer grain than the state level could help in determining strategic places to expand youth programs.

One method of measuring outreach would be to conduct a survey of a random subsample of the population, including questions on awareness and impressions of various aspects of military outreach programs. However, such a survey would have to be quite extensive and therefore very costly to produce estimates that are stable at the local level (and local estimates would be required to determine the extent to which existing programs appear to influence awareness and impressions).[1]

Existing surveys could also be adapted to serve this purpose. While the GSS survey that we utilize is fairly small in scope, it is possible that additional analyses with

---

[1] For example, the ACS can be used to produce estimates down to the census block level; this survey includes observations on about 3 million persons (about 1 percent of the U.S. population) yearly. Such a survey is, of course, extremely costly.

this data source could produce valuable information about the factors that influence military confidence, and especially the factors that are related to changes in the public's confidence in the military. Because our analyses of access to youth programs and military confidence was at the state level, sample size limitations made it difficult to do a thorough investigation into the individual-level factors that are related to military confidence. Other data could potentially be used to examine this in the future. The JAMRS Youth Poll or Influencer Poll could also provide useful information. These polls are relatively small, however; while they may be able to provide helpful information on trends over time, they lack the sample size necessary to produce more precise estimates of variation by geography. Another option, which has been utilized by a few STARBASE programs in the past, is to track STARBASE participants well beyond the program to measure differences in high school course completion, college attendance, majoring or working in STEM-related fields, and so on.

The methods used in this report were descriptive or involved regression models. Future work could consider experimental or quasi-experimental methods to examine the relationship between outreach efforts and longer-term outcomes. One possible study design would take advantage of STARBASE program openings or closings in an area and use a predesign and postdesign model to examine change in these areas.

In this project we have documented the number and type of students who are served by STARBASE, but we have also focused on several aspects of outreach. We find that individual STARBASE programs have outreach efforts that focus on building relationships with local businesses and organizations; this appears appropriate. However, we also find evidence that all of DoD's youth programs act as a type of military outreach; this suggests that managing the placement of the youth programs as a group (rather than making individual placement decisions without regard to the locations of other types of youth programs) could serve to increase military outreach. The pattern between military confidence and the locations of youth programs suggests that STARBASE and ChalleNGe are located in areas with slightly lower levels of confidence than are JROTC programs. This type of placement could be optimal, but determining optimal location of future programs requires first measuring the outreach effects of these programs and then strategically placing programs in areas that lack other outreach efforts or have lower-than-average levels of military confidence.

Data and Methods

Many of our analyses are based on a master data file constructed at the school district level. In this appendix we document the sources of the variables included in the file and include some descriptive information on the variables; we also provide additional information on the data utilized in our analyses.

Neighborhood Data

Neighborhood contextual data come from the ACS. Data was pulled from the NCES Education Demographic and Geographic Estimates website, which has ACS data at the school district level ready for easy downloading. We include all school districts in the 2009–2013 ACS five-year estimates data. School districts include elementary, secondary, and unified school districts. Counts are based on the total population in the school districts and exclude information on charter or institutional schools.

School Data

School-specific data come from the NCES CCD. CCD school-level data from the years 2008–2014 were used to make a school district year file (as more recent data were not yet available when we carried out our analyses). The data include regular schools and charter schools. For our analyses of which districts are served by STARBASE programs, we limited our sample to districts with fifth graders. Graduation/dropout rates were based on information included in the NCES restricted file; from these data we formed a variable to indicate the districts with the highest dropout rates. The variable identifies the quartile of high school students who attend schools in districts with the highest dropout rates.

Crime Data

The crime data come from the Uniform Crime Reporting Program, which is maintained by the Inter-University Consortium for Political and Social Research and include counts of crimes and arrests for violent crimes and property crimes reported by law agencies at the county level. To get reliable 2012 county population counts needed for the denominator of the crime rates estimates, we used the 2012 Population Estimate Program residential population data file from the U.S. Census Bureau website. These 2012 population estimates were merged by county according to the Federal Information Processing Standards and used for the denominator in crime rates.

To assign a school district code for linkage to the NCES data, we used information provided by NCES. This created data that were roughly consistent with the neighborhood/ACS data (see above). For New York City schools, we aggregated the data for all the counties that make up the New York City school system. We did the same for Hawaii, where all schools across all counties are in one school district that is headed by the State Department of Education. We also aggregated each independent city in Virginia with its surrounding county to get a full county crime estimate (in Virginia, some cities are independent from the counties that surround them).

The crime data use slightly older county codes than the NCES data, so county changes in Alaska that occurred between 2000 and 2010 are not accounted for. In some counties, not all agencies reported crime statistics. For these cases, crime rates are imputed. If a county was completely missing information on crime, numbers were imputed based on state figures and using the county's proportion of the state population as a weight; if all counties reported data, there was no imputation.

Factor Analyses, Measure of Disadvantage

Table A.1 lists the measures that we tested when forming our measure of disadvantage. To obtain this measure, we did an exploratory factor analysis with varimax rotation; a scree plot suggested a natural break at three factors. Those measures that loaded onto the primary factor with loadings of 0.3 or better were retained in our measure of disadvantage. The alpha (reliability) coefficient for the final measures in the scale was 0.8263. Those measures are indicated with X's below.

STARBASE Data

To determine school districts served by a STARBASE program, we compiled data from annual reports on program name, location, start date, and a few other items. In matching these to the ACS school district data from the NCES website, we found that

Table A.1
Neighborhood Measures of Disadvantage Considered for Final Factor Score

	Included in Final Factor
Average household size	
Percentage under age 18	
Percentage 65 and older	
Percentage in same residence as last year (residential stability)	X
Percentage on public assistance	X
Percentage below poverty threshold	X
Percentage unemployed	X
Percentage in professional/management occupations	
Percentage with no vehicle	X
Percentage with less than a high school education	X
Percentage with a BA degree or higher	
Percentage of female-headed households with children under age 18	X
Percentage of household with >1 person per room (household crowding)	X
Median household income	X
Median home value	

250 of the 266 school districts were included in the ACS data and the other 16 school districts were school types that were not included in the NCES ACS-based files. These 16 districts are therefore missing neighborhood data.

Applicants/Accession Data

Applicant/Accessions counts came from the United States Military Entrance Processing Command file. Applicant/accession counts were pooled from FY2011 to FY2015 and aggregated by the home zip code of the applicant. Counts were merged with school district data using information provided by NCES. In merging the school district level applicant/accession counts with the NCES ACS data, we treated school districts with no match as districts that had no applicants/accessions in the FY2011–FY2015 period. In the applicant/accession models, for school districts that are not unified, we further rolled up to one aggregated primary-secondary school district.

JROTC Data

Our sponsor provided a list of schools with JROTC programs. We used information provided by NCES to merge these data with the school district data. There are a number of private, military, and other nontraditional schools in the data, which were assigned to their nearest district.

Recruiter Data

Recruiter locations were ascertained from the recruiting websites of the U.S. Air Force, U.S. Army, and U.S. Navy.[1] A list of every recruiter address in the United States was created and placed on a map using geographic information system software. These locations were overlaid on the 2015 School District Boundary files created by the U.S. Census Bureau (undated). To calculate the ultimate variable, a "recruiter influence score," a 30-mile buffer was added around each recruiter location as the farthest distance that a potential applicant would travel to visit a recruiter. The overlap between each school district and recruiter buffer was then calculated as a fraction of the school district area. The recruiter overlap fractions for all school districts were then added together to create the ultimate variable. For example, if a school district was half covered by a single recruiter, the score would be 0.5. If a district was one-fourth covered by one recruiter, and half covered by another, the score would be 0.75, even if the recruiter buffers overlapped. The variable was calculated for each service individually, and then as a total military recruiter score.

Military Influence Data

The location of all domestic military facilities came from Google Maps (undated). The population of military installations came from a table in *2015 Demographics: Profile of the Military Community*, published by the DoD Office of the Deputy Assistant Secretary of Defense for Military Community and Family Policy (undated). Any military facility or installation not in this report has a servicemember sponsor population of under 100. Two measures were created from these data: The first records whether a school district has a military facility in it, based on overlaying the Google Maps data with school district boundaries using geographic information system software. The second variable is a measure of military influence, which uses the population of the installations as a proxy for extent of influence in a community. Variable buffers were

---

[1]   For the recruiter sites, see U.S. Air Force (undated); U.S. Army (undated); and U.S. Navy (undated).

created around the zip codes of each military facility. The largest buffer, corresponding to the highest population, was set at 30 miles. The size of the buffers was directly scaled to the population, the lowest value being 0 for those facilities with no recorded population. The overlap between the zip codes (with buffer) and school districts was then calculated in the same way that the recruiter influence score was for recruiter data. In total, there were 324 facilities located in 346 districts; a few facilities crossed school district borders. There were 2,807 recruiting stations.

Google Analytics Data

We used Google Analytics data (specifically, information provided by the Google Trends tool) to determine how widespread key searches were. The data span the time period 2004–2015 (Google Search data are not available prior to 2004), and offer the advantage of capturing all relevant searches that took place through Google, but the data are aggregated and anonymized.[2] Therefore it is not possible to determine who was searching. Additionally, the Google Trends tool reports search levels in a normed fashion. Nonetheless, these data offer a unique source of information, and it is possible to compare the relative numbers of searches across different terms. Is it also worth noting that search data have been found to be correlated with a number of relevant outcomes; examples include influenza (Ginsberg et al., 2009, but see also Lazer et al., 2014, for key caveats), unemployment figures (Ettredge, Gerdes, and Karuga, 2005), and Army accessions (Jahedi, Wenger, and Young, 2016).

Facebook Data

We used simple tabulations of the number of STARBASE Facebook pages, as well as the content on these pages as of October 2015.

JAMRS Data

We also analyzed data on 1,188 military influencers from JAMRS. The JAMRS Influencer Poll is a quarterly telephone survey designed to "measure an influencer's likelihood to recommend military service to youth and to support a youth's decision to join

---

[2]   There are other search engines, but Google appears to dominate among those performing web searches; see Purcell, Brenner, and Rainie (2012). More recent analyses suggest that Google continues to dominate; see, e.g., Matsa, Mitchell, and Stocking (2017).

the Military" (Carvalho et al., 2008, p. 1). Analyses presented here primarily focus on a wave of the survey collected in the spring of 2013 that includes additional battery of questions relating to influencer social media usage, with several analyses comparing responses on specific questions across the 2013, 2014, and 2015 surveys to look at trends over time. These data are not available with geographic indicators and are thus not pooled with the other data in the study but instead analyzed separately.

Descriptive Statistics and Regression Results, Military Applicants and Accessions

In creating our regression model, we started with an extensive list of variables to test for possible inclusion as they could be connected to the number and quality of applicants and accessions. The variables are as follows, with the ones included in the final model highlighted in **boldface**:

- **violent crime rate**
- **property crime rate**
- **neighborhood disadvantage (described in Appendix A)**
- **percentage of fifth graders in Title I schools**
- percentage of schools with Title I programs
- percentage of fifth graders who receive free or reduced-price school lunches
- percentage of African American and Hispanic residents in the school district
- **percentage of non-Hispanic black residents in the neighborhood**
- **percentage of Hispanic residents in the neighborhood**
- **percentage of foreign-born residents in neighborhood**
- percentage of non–native English speakers in the neighborhood
- school districts in the top 10% of dropout rates
- school districts in the first quartile of dropout rates
- school districts below the mean of dropout rates
- **school districts in the top quartile of dropout rates**
- **recruiter influence score**
- total JROTC programs per 10,000 students
- school districts having JROTC programs
- military influence score (the proportion of the school district living within 30 miles of a military recruiter)
- **military presence**
- **percentage of residents who are in the military**
- **percentage of residents who are veterans**
- school districts having STARBASE programs
- **school districts having youth programs**

- number of youth programs
- population density
- **census division**
- state
- region.

We tested the correlation of the variables to avoid having two variables with high correlation in our model. Percentages of Hispanic and non-Hispanic black residents were combined into one variable because they were highly correlated with each other and with several disadvantage factors. When testing a model with all school variables held constant, the school disadvantage variable that performed the best was percentage of fifth graders in Title I schools, so that was retained. The percentage of non–native English speakers was also removed because of high correlation with the percentage of foreign-born residents. There were four variables relevant to dropout rates, which were tested in the same way as the school disadvantage factors; the one that performed the best was a school district being in the top quartile of dropout rates. Both military presence and influence were tested, and presence was more significant. Lastly, we had a number of geographic variables and chose to keep the census division variable, as it provided the highest level of significance.

The variables that remained in our model are shown in Table B.1. We suspected that relationships were different among urban, suburban, and rural districts, and examining descriptive statistics showed that to be the case.

Because of these differences, we modeled each outcome separately for urban, suburban, and rural school districts.[1] The results of this preferred specification appear in Tables B.2 and B.3. In Table B.4, we present results from an alternate specification of high-quality accessions.

Table B.1
Descriptive Statistics, by Urbanicity of School District

Continuous Variables	Urban (n = 2,814)			Suburban (n = 2,354)			Rural (n = 4,928)		
	Min	Mean	Max	Min	Mean	Max	Min	Mean	Max
Violent crime rate	0.00	280.43	1,793.37	7.42	323.92	1,745.27	0.00	217.97	1,745.27
Property crime rate	0.00	2,481.18	7,017.90	165.00	2,514.43	6,911.12	0.00	2,022.32	6,845.13

---

[1] In the CCD, schools are classified as being located in a city, suburb, or rural area. We classified districts as urban, suburban, or rural if the largest number of students attended schools in these respective areas.

Table B.1—Continued

Continuous Variables	Urban (n = 2,814)			Suburban (n = 2,354)			Rural (n = 4,928)		
	Min	Mean	Max	Min	Mean	Max	Min	Mean	Max
Percentage foreign born	0.00	6.38	52.90	0.00	10.27	63.70	0.00	2.92	50.90
Percentage in the military	0.00	0.39	69.90	0.00	0.28	79.70	0.00	0.12	28.20
Percentage veterans	1.10	9.90	34.30	0.80	8.71	34.50	0.40	10.76	28.60
Neighborhood disadvantage	−1.39	0.38	5.09	−1.61	−0.26	4.83	−1.69	−0.05	6.51
Percentage fifth graders in Title I schools	0.00	0.73	1.00	0.00	0.40	1.00	0.00	0.71	1.00
Percentage black and Hispanic	0.00	20.69	98.20	0.10	18.51	99.60	0.00	10.54	99.80
Population density	0.62	448.72	13,522.10	2.07	1,461.05	40,110.99	0.01	45.64	1,416.88
Military influence score	0.00	0.02	1.00	0.00	0.02	1.01	0.00	0.00	1.00
Number of JROTC programs per 10k students	0.00	0.27	308.85	0.00	0.18	60.24	0.00	0.01	6.76
Number of youth programs	0.00	0.27	3.00	0.00	0.25	2.00	0.00	0.10	2.00
Total recruiter score	0.00	5.31	82.74	0.00	21.39	81.92	0.00	3.35	57.46
Accessions per population	0.00	0.00	0.01	0.00	0.00	0.01	0.00	0.00	0.01
Applicants per population	0.00	0.00	0.02	0.00	0.00	0.02	0.00	0.00	0.03
Percentage high-quality accessions	0.00	0.75	1.00	0.00	0.78	1.00	0.00	0.74	1.00

Categorical Variables	n [x = 0]	n [x = 1]	% [x = 1]	n [x = 0]	n [x = 1]	% [x = 1]	n [x = 0]	n [x = 1]	% [x = 1]
No crime data	2,814	0	0%	2,354	0	0%	4,924	4	0%
In top quartile of dropout data	2,162	652	23%	1,333	1,021	43%	3,344	1,584	32%
No dropout data	2,685	129	5%	2,208	146	6%	4,638	290	6%
Excluding Alaska	2,807	7	0%	2,354	0	0%	4,909	19	0%

Table B.1—Continued

Categorical Variables	n [x = 0]	n [x = 1]	% [x = 1]	n [x = 0]	n [x = 1]	% [x = 1]	n [x = 0]	n [x = 1]	% [x = 1]
Has JROTC	2,162	652	23%	1,826	528	22%	4,543	385	8%
Has ChalleNGe program	2,789	25	1%	2,350	4	0%	4,919	9	0%
Has STARBASE program	2,730	84	3%	2,305	49	2%	4,851	77	2%
Has youth program	2,121	693	25%	1,803	551	23%	4,477	451	9%
Military presence	2,735	79	3%	2,301	53	2%	4,913	15	0%
Has recruiter	277	2,537	90%	2	2,352	100%	756	4,172	85%
Census division									
East North Central	2,224	590	21%	1,779	575	24%	3,891	1,037	21%
East South Central	2,614	200	7%	2,283	71	3%	4,635	293	6%
Mid-Atlantic	2,579	235	8%	1,654	700	30%	4,451	477	10%
Mountain	2,571	243	9%	2,296	58	2%	4,603	325	7%
New England	2,717	97	3%	2,047	307	13%	4,706	222	5%
Pacific	2,480	334	12%	2,122	232	10%	4,659	269	5%
South Atlantic	2,615	199	7%	2,224	130	6%	4,590	338	7%
West North Central	2,378	436	15%	2,232	122	5%	3,949	979	20%
West South Central	2,334	480	17%	2,195	159	7%	3,940	988	20%

Table B.2
Coefficients and *P*-Values from Regression Models Predicting Number of Applicants (per 1,000 people)

	Applicants per Population					
Dataset ≥	Urban		Suburban		Rural	
Variable	Coefficient	*P*-Value	Coefficient	*P*-Value	Coefficient	*P*-Value
(Intercept)	1.03E-03*	1.24E-13	4.33E-04*	3.43E-03	1.69E-03*	1.22E-42
Violent crime rate	4.38E-08	7.87E-01	−8.65E-08	5.65E-01	−5.79E-08	7.47E-01

Table B.2—Continued

Dataset ≥	Applicants per Population					
	Urban		Suburban		Rural	
Variable	Coefficient	P-Value	Coefficient	P-Value	Coefficient	P-Value
Property crime rate	7.29E-08*	9.95E-03	1.19E-08	7.40E-01	1.61E-07*	1.85E-08
Dropout rate in the top quartile	6.91E-05	2.60E-01	−1.12E-04*	3.35E-02	1.16E-05	8.24E-01
No dropout data	2.46E-04*	3.24E-02	8.04E-05	3.85E-01	2.42E-04*	1.78E-02
Recruiter influence score	1.47E-05*	8.13E-05	8.86E-07	5.98E-01	4.48E-05*	4.30E-13
Percentage foreign born	−2.73E-05*	2.06E-07	−9.89E-06*	9.83E-03	−3.72E-05*	2.47E-07
Percentage in the military	3.98E-05*	2.67E-04	−3.76E-05*	6.19E-04	1.46E-04*	9.20E-05
Percentage veterans	2.13E-04*	1.99E-86	2.87E-04*	1.01E-130	1.34E-04*	1.62E-50
Neighborhood disadvantage	7.85E-05*	3.76E-02	9.12E-05*	3.01E-02	6.76E-05	5.19E-02
Percentage of fifth graders in Title I Schools	1.33E-04	6.21E-02	9.27E-05	1.84E-01	2.55E-04*	2.77E-05
Has youth program	1.49E-04*	2.11E-02	2.42E-04*	3.28E-05	−9.37E-05	3.16E-01
Military presence	5.03E-04*	2.04E-03	1.02E-04	5.12E-01	1.00E-03*	3.02E-02
Division: East South Central	−1.36E-04	2.08E-01	5.88E-05	6.51E-01	−2.72E-04*	1.95E-02
Division: Mid-Atlantic	−2.08E-04*	2.91E-02	−3.98E-04*	3.43E-10	−8.70E-05	3.31E-01
Division: Mountain	−5.12E-04*	3.56E-07	−1.22E-04	3.90E-01	2.95E-05	7.85E-01
Division: New England	−4.51E-04*	9.64E-04	−5.05E-04*	4.31E-11	−4.51E-04*	2.10E-04
Division: Pacific	1.07E-04	2.88E-01	1.88E-04*	3.24E-02	−1.38E-04	2.50E-01
Division: South Atlantic	5.95E-04*	6.89E-08	2.52E-04*	2.14E-02	3.06E-04*	9.71E-03
Division: West North Central	−4.66E-04*	5.11E-09	−2.58E-05	8.00E-01	−6.09E-04*	1.14E-16
Division: West South Central	1.77E-04*	3.99E-02	3.94E-04*	7.82E-05	3.43E-04*	1.66E-05
Percentage black and Hispanic	1.34E-05*	3.01E-12	2.61E-05*	6.30E-41	1.41E-05*	1.49E-10
Multiple R-Squared	0.349		0.5547		0.1608	

NOTE: Results of linear regression models predicting number of applicants as a function of school and neighborhood characteristics. Coefficients marked with * indicate a $p < 0.05$ result unlikely to have occurred by chance.

Table B.3
Coefficients and *P*-Values from Regression Models Predicting Number of Accessions (per 1,000 people)

Data Set ≥	Accessions per Population					
	Urban		Suburban		Rural	
Variable	Coefficient	*P*-Value	Coefficient	*P*-Value	Coefficient	*P*-Value
(Intercept)	6.13E-04*	2.47E-14	3.77E-04*	3.98E-06	9.49E-04*	1.53E-37
Violent crime rate	9.45E-08	3.12E-01	1.45E-08	8.61E-01	6.80E-08	5.29E-01
Property crime rate	1.96E-08	2.29E-01	−1.76E-08	3.77E-01	5.52E-08*	1.36E-03
Dropout rate in the top quartile	5.13E-05	1.46E-01	−8.13E-05*	5.22E-03	−4.20E-06	8.94E-01
No dropout data	1.03E-04	1.18E-01	−7.83E-06	8.78E-01	−4.50E-05	4.64E-01
Recruiter influence score	4.54E-06*	3.45E-02	−1.10E-06	2.36E-01	2.59E-05*	3.13E-12
Percentage foreign born	−9.63E-06*	1.42E-03	−3.03E-06	1.52E-01	−1.57E-05*	2.88E-04
Percentage in the military	2.50E-05*	6.98E-05	−2.06E-05*	6.85E-04	9.10E-05*	4.79E-05
Percentage veterans	1.19E-04*	1.26E-81	1.49E-04*	4.73E-117	7.47E-05*	1.10E-43
Neighborhood disadvantage	1.84E-05	3.98E-01	7.71E-06	7.40E-01	−1.97E-05	3.46E-01
Percentage of fifth graders in Title I schools	9.01E-05*	2.82E-02	5.13E-05	1.83E-01	1.62E-04*	9.77E-06
Has youth program	4.87E-05	1.89E-01	1.24E-04*	1.09E-04	−6.14E-05	2.74E-01
Military presence	1.95E-04*	3.75E-02	7.97E-06	9.26E-01	3.01E-04	2.79E-01
Division: East South Central	−1.73E-04*	5.38E-03	−1.03E-04	1.51E-01	−2.63E-04*	1.77E-04
Division: Mid-Atlantic	−1.82E-04*	9.53E-04	−2.70E-04*	1.55E-14	−8.54E-05	1.13E-01
Division: Mountain	−2.38E-04*	3.78E-05	−2.37E-06	9.76E-01	−8.09E-05	2.14E-01
Division: New England	−2.25E-04*	4.30E-03	−2.93E-04*	3.93E-12	−1.78E-04*	1.48E-02
Division: Pacific	1.30E-04*	2.51E-02	1.70E-04*	4.86E-04	−7.61E-06	9.16E-01
Division: South Atlantic	1.23E-04	5.16E-02	1.15E-04	5.79E-02	1.18E-05	8.68E-01
Division: West North Central	−2.79E-04*	1.22E-09	−4.26E-05	4.49E-01	−3.73E-04*	3.52E-17
Division: West South Central	−9.64E-06	8.46E-01	1.97E-04*	3.36E-04	5.38E-05	2.61E-01
Percentage black and Hispanic	1.88E-06	8.90E-02	8.29E-06*	5.54E-15	4.64E-06*	4.31E-04
Multiple *R*-Squared	0.3006		0.4984		0.1167	

NOTE: Results of linear regression models predicting number of applicants as a function of school and neighborhood characteristics. Coefficients marked with * indicate a $p < 0.05$ result unlikely to have occurred by chance.

Table B.4
Coefficients and *P*-Values from Regression Models Predicting Percentage of High-Quality Accessions (per 1,000 people)

	High-Quality Accessions per Population					
	Urban		Suburban		Rural	
Dataset ≥						
Variable	Coefficient	P-Value	Coefficient	P-Value	Coefficient	P-Value
(Intercept)	7.60E-0*	0.00E+00	8.05E-01*	0.00E+00	7.40E-01*	0.00E+00
Violent crime rate	−2.54E-05	7.15E-02	−1.58E-05	1.94E-01	−4.64E-05*	4.03E-02
Property crime rate	9.00E-06*	2.53E-04	−2.03E-06	4.85E-01	4.27E-06	2.36E-01
Dropout rate in the top quartile	1.48E-03	7.81E-01	3.74E-03	3.79E-01	−2.49E-03	7.06E-01
No dropout data	−4.53E-03	6.50E-01	1.02E-03	8.91E-01	−3.04E-02*	1.81E-02
Recruiter influence score	1.39E-04	6.69E-01	−2.37E-04*	8.03E-02	2.17E-03*	5.26E-03
Percentage foreign born	2.31E-03*	4.09E-07	8.13E-04*	8.49E-03	3.30E-03*	2.73E-04
Percentage in the military	−1.11E-03	2.41E-01	−9.26E-04	2.95E-01	−1.96E-04	9.67E-01
Percentage Veteran	5.25E-04	5.63E-01	−1.07E-03	2.29E-01	1.39E-03	2.13E-01
Neighborhood disadvantage	−3.62E-02*	1.05E-27	−3.20E-02*	8.22E-21	−3.67E-02*	6.49E-17
Percentage of fifth graders in Title I schools	−1.22E-02*	4.94E-02	−1.99E-02*	4.02E-04	−5.08E-03	5.07E-01
Has youth program	−7.24E-03	1.95E-01	7.05E-03	1.33E-01	1.20E-03	9.18E-01
Military presence	1.12E-02	4.28E-01	−1.96E-05	9.99E-01	−2.61E-03	9.64E-01
Division: East South Central	−3.33E-02*	3.78E-04	−2.07E-02*	4.87E-02	−3.09E-02*	3.50E-02
Division: Mid-Atlantic	1.43E-02	8.41E-02	2.76E-03	5.88E-01	−4.60E-03	6.83E-01
Division: Mountain	2.54E-02*	3.59E-03	3.94E-02*	5.97E-04	3.77E-03	7.82E-01
Division: New England	6.90E-03	5.61E-01	2.12E-02*	5.53E-04	1.44E-02	3.47E-01
Division: Pacific	1.77E-02*	4.41E-02	5.62E-02*	3.65E-15	1.90E-02	2.09E-01
Division: South Atlantic	−3.02E-02*	1.57E-03	1.05E-02	2.33E-01	−2.10E-02	1.60E-01
Division: West North Central	−3.66E-03	5.96E-01	5.71E-03	4.87E-01	−6.23E-03	5.00E-01
Division: West South Central	−1.16E-02	1.20E-01	3.37E-02*	2.79E-05	−1.93E-02	5.45E-02
Percentage black and Hispanic	−1.12E-03*	2.33E-11	−1.43E-03*	4.04E-20	−1.38E-03*	6.31E-07
Multiple *R*-Squared	0.2339		0.3405		0.06714	

NOTE: Results of linear regression models predicting any high-quality accessions as a function of school and neighborhood characteristics. Coefficients marked with * indicate a *p* < 0.05 result unlikely to have occurred by chance.

Supplemental Influencer Media Impressions and Online Engagement

This appendix contains additional supplemental information and analyses to support the results presented in Chapter Six. The focus is on the types of media that influencers use to gather information and impressions of military service.

Media Source Impressions

The questions from the JAMRS Influencer Poll used in the analyses in Chapter Six were as follows:

- Impression: "People get their impressions about the Military from many sources. From what types of people or sources of information do you get the majority of your impressions about the Military? MARK ALL THAT APPLY"
- For those impressions selected:
  - Positivity: Was impression from [source] "Completely Negative 01, Mostly Negative 02, Neither Positive nor Negative 03, Mostly Positive 04, Completely Positive 05"
  - Trust: "Please indicate how much you trust the information that you have received about the U.S. Military from each of the sources listed below. Don't trust at all 01, Trust very little 02, Trust somewhat 03, Trust a lot 04, Trust completely 05"

Table C.1 presents the raw data used to produce Figure 6.1. Statistical significance compares noted values to those of social media for the appropriate column.

Figure C.1 presents the changes in influencer impressions over time. Most changes were relatively modest, but the proportion of influencers who reported drawing impressions about the military from social media increased substantially between 2013 and 2015.

Table C.1
Sources of Media Impressions

Media Source	Influenced Impression Percent (N using)	Percent of Those Used: Positive Impression	Percent of Those Used: Negative Impression	Percent of Those Used: Trust Source
Advertising (AD)	19.28% (229)	75.55%*	3.06%	15.28%
Movies (MV)	21.38% (254)	45.28%	14.17%	7.48%*
News websites (NW)	19.11% (227)	32.16%	21.59%	16.74%
Other websites (OW)	5.05% (60)	33.33%	21.67%	15.00%
Radio (RD)	5.81% (69)	43.48%	2.90%	21.74%
Social media (SM)	9.85% (117)	36.75%	17.09%	16.24%
Television (TV)	41.92% (498)	45.58%	12.65%	17.67%
Things you've read (TR)	40.82% (485)	41.86%	15.88%	23.09%
Video games (VG)	2.86% (32)	41.18%	17.65%	14.71%

NOTE: n = 1,188.
* $p < 0.01$.

Figure C.1
Influencer Impression Sources over Time

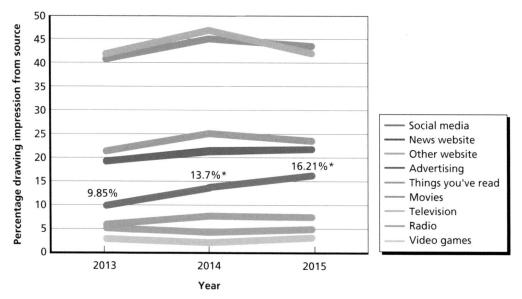

NOTE: News websites and advertising track nearly identically across all years. * $p < 0.05$.
RAND RR2160OSD-C.1

Online Engagement with DoD Sources

Survey Questions

For the Air Force, Army, Coast Guard, Navy, and Marine Corps, influencers were asked:

- "Have you visited a website for any of the following military branches to gather information about [text alternation: "your child's" if xgroup = 1–4; "your grand-child's" if xgroup = 5; "a young person's" if xgroup = 6] future options?"
- "Have you ever visited a social media (e.g., Facebook, Twitter, YouTube, Flickr) page for the _____?"

Answering yes for any service was counted as this type of engagement with online DoD content.

Next we modeled influencer engagement as a function of several key variables: demographics, social media usage, and existing attitudes toward the military. We used logistic regressions, with either engaging with DoD websites or DoD social media platforms as the dependent variable. All models utilize sampling weights available in the JAMRS Influencer Poll. Demographics examined include age, gender, influencer type, race/ethnicity, census region of residence, education, income, prior military service, frequency of social media usage, willingness to recommend military service, and knowledge of the military as predictors.[1] Of these, only age and prior military service remained in play with the use of sampling weights. Regression results appear in Tables C.2 and C.3.

Two key influencer characteristics examined relate to their attitude toward and knowledge of the military. We first examined the willingness of influencers to recommend military service to the youth they influence. This measure captures influencers who state they would be likely or very likely to recommend military service to those youth. The second measure captures influencer's self-reported knowledge of the military. These two items reflect a general affinity with the military, either in knowledge of what service entails and/or a willingness to recommend service to youth. We expect both of these factors to be associated with higher online engagement with

---

[1] Social media usage is a factor derived from an exploratory factor analysis of how frequently in a given week an influencer has used blogs, discussion boards/forums, Facebook, Google Plus, Instagram, LinkedIn, Myspace, Pinterest, Reddit (or other social news sites), Tumblr, Twitter, Wikipedia, Yelp (or other social rating sites), or YouTube. After an orthogonal rotation, all items save Facebook use loaded positively on a single factor that we call general social media use. This factor is top coded at the ninety-ninth percentile to address a handful of extreme values.

Table C.2
Logistic Regression of Military Website Engagement

	(1)	(2)	(3)
Demographics			
Social media use	2.043*	2.053*	1.999*
	(2.17)	(2.20)	(2.12)
Age in years	0.977**	0.976**	
	(−2.62)	(−2.72)	
Young (under 45 years old)			1.687*
			(2.53)
Military-Specific			
Veteran	0.865		0.812
	(−0.47)		(−0.69)
Recommend service	2.378***	2.327***	2.354***
	(4.05)	(3.88)	(4.04)
Knowledge of military	1.644***	1.603***	1.652***
	(3.59)	(3.83)	(3.66)
n	1157	1157	1157
Pseudo R^2	0.094	0.094	0.090

NOTE: Exponentiated coefficients; z-statistics in parentheses.
* $p < 0.05$.
** $p < 0.01$.
*** $p < 0.001$.

DoD content.[2] Table C.4 presents descriptive statistics for these measures; we examine these measures in more detail below.

Characteristics of Influences with Online DoD Engagement

Influencers who report online contact with DoD sources share several similar features. These influencers tend to be more frequent social media users who already have some level of comfort or familiarity with military service. Figure C.2 highlights key results from these models. For each point, increases in social media usage on a scale from roughly −2 to 2 increases the chance that an influencer will have viewed a military website by 104.3 percent, holding other characteristics constant. There is no significant change for accessing military social media engagement, but the observed

---

[2]   This measure is a summary scale that asks respondents to rate their knowledge of the requirements to join the military, the careers available in the military, educational benefits available in the military, the military lifestyle, and health care benefits available in the military. Higher scores indicate more self-reported knowledge.

Table C.3
Logistic Regression of Social Media Engagement

	(1)	(2)	(3)
Demographics			
Social media use	1.975 (1.54)	1.901 (1.48)	1.957 (1.54)
Age in years	0.990 (−0.70)	0.992 (−0.56)	
Young (under 45 years old)			1.353 (0.95)
Military-Specific			
Veteran	1.602 (1.07)		1.577 (1.06)
Recommend service	1.728 (1.72)	1.874* (1.98)	1.723 (1.72)
Knowledge of military	1.549 (1.59)	1.702** (2.13)	1.553 (1.60)
n	1157	1157	1157
Pseudo R^2	0.074	0.070	0.075

NOTE: Exponentiated coefficients; z statistics in parentheses.
* $p < 0.05$.
** $p < 0.001$.

Table C.4
Descriptive Statistics

Measure	Mean	Standard Deviation	Minimum	Maximum
Has visited military website	0.18	0.39	0	1
Has visited military social media	0.07	0.26	0	1
Prior service	0.16	0.36	0	1
Age	50.26	12.88	25	86
Would recommend military service	0.43	0.49	0	1
Knowledge of military	3.31	0.96	1	5
Social media use (factor)	−0.05	0.33	−2.21	2.07

Figure C.2
Change in Engaging Online DoD Content by Key Variables

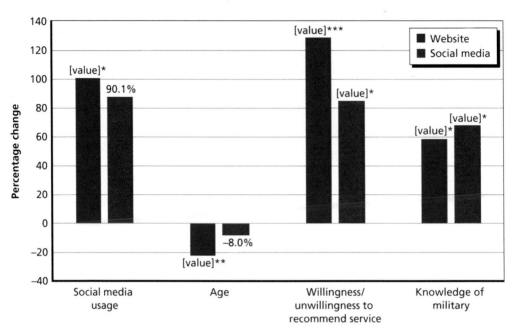

NOTE: * $p < 0.05$; ** $p < 0.01$; *** $p < 0.001$.
RAND RR2160OSD-C.2

effect is in the same direction. Given that far fewer influences report engagement with military social media generally, this may be a lack of statistical power in the analyses. As expected, those influencers who use social media frequently are more likely to have online engagement with DoD content. If nothing else, this relationship is indicative of the increased time these influencers spend online. Even as more frequent social media users report increased engagement with DoD content, older influencers report less contact. Holding constant other characteristics, increasing age by ten years decreases the chance an influencer will visit a military website by 23 percent. Again, the relationship for military social media is in the same direction but is not statistically significant.

Other key influencer characteristics are their attitudes toward and knowledge of military service. As each of these factors increases, influences are significantly more likely to visit both military websites and social media. Influencers who are willing to recommend service visit military websites at a rate 132.7 percent greater, and military social media at 87.4 percent greater, than influencers who are not willing to recommend service. Similarly increasing influencer knowledge of the military by one point increases their chance of visiting a military website by 60.3 percent, and social media

Figure C.3
Probability of Influencer Engagement with Military Website

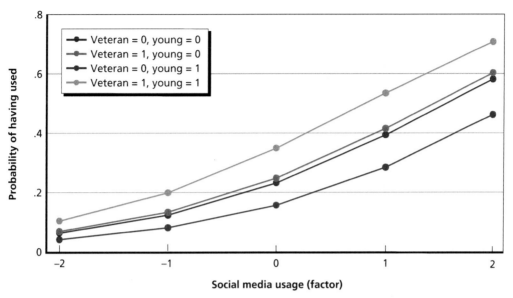

RAND RR2160OSD-C.3

by 70.2 percent. Taken together, influencers who are more comfortable with military service are more likely to engage with online DoD content, be it websites or social media. It is also possible that engaging with DoD content online increases influencer comfort with the military. Given the nature of the data available, we are unable to fully distinguish between these possibilities, but it seems more plausible that comfort leads to more engagement rather than limited visits to a website dramatically changing views of the military.

In addition to examining these factors individually, we also examine key factors in an interactive fashion to allow relationships between factors. Figures C.3 and C.4 present the probability of an influencer having engaged with a type of online content based on the influencer's age, social media usage, and prior service.[3] Age is once again split between influencers older or younger than 45.

The probability of engaging with a military website increases with an influencer's social media usage. Being a veteran also increases the probability of visiting a military website, as does being younger than 45 years old. Notably, the effects for age and prior

---

[3] We focus on prior service over other attitudes/knowledge items above to mitigate the causality question between these items and online engagement. Prior service has similar relationships to these outcomes, and it seems less likely that veterans are drawing their comfort with the military from visiting websites or social media given their extensive firsthand experience with military service.

Figure C.4
Probability of Influencer Engagement with Military Social Media

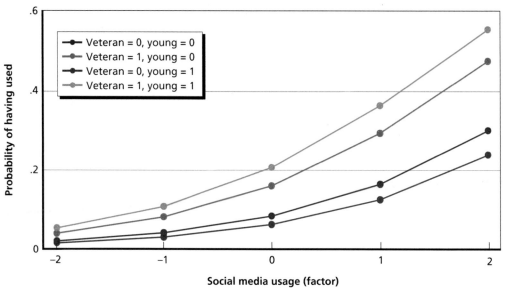

service are of the same magnitude, as shown by younger nonveterans visiting military websites at a similar rate as older veterans. In this case there is no significant effect of age on social media engagement. This reinforces results throughout Chapter Six suggesting that age does not necessarily lead to increased DoD and military social media engagement.

Bibliography

Associated Press–NORC Center for Public Affairs Research, "Confidence in Institutions: Trends in Americans' Attitudes Toward Government, Media, and Business," undated. As of July 12, 2018: http://www.apnorc.org/projects/Pages/HTML Reports/confidence-in-institutions-trends-in -americans-attitudes-toward-government-media-and-business0310-2333.aspx

Burk, James, "The Military's Presence in American Society, 1950–2000," in Peter D. Fever and Richard H. Kohn, eds., *Soldiers and Civilians*, Cambridge, Mass.: MIT Press, 2001, 247–74.

Carter, Ash, "Remarks on 'Forging Two New Links to the Force of the Future,'" U.S. Department of Defense, November 1, 2016. As of July 10, 2018: https://www.defense.gov/News/Speeches/Speech-View/Article/995929/remarks-on-forging-two -new-links-to-the-force-of-the-future/

Carvalho, Ricardo S., Scott R. Turner, Sean M. Marsh, Tiffany Yanosky, Andrea B. Zucker, and Matt Boehmer, *Department of Defense Influencer Poll Wave 10—June 2008: Overview Report*, Arlington, Va.: U.S. Department of Defense, Defense Human Resources Activity, Joint Advertising Market & Research Studies, December 2008. As of July 12, 2018: https://jamrs.defense.gov/Portals/20/Documents/Influencer_Poll_10.pdf

Chang, Joy, "Bridging the Racial Gap in STEM Education," National Action Council on Minorities in Engineering, November 8, 2015. As of September 10, 2017: http://www.nacme.org/news/articles/170-bridging-the-racial-gap-in-stem-education

Change the Equation, "Design Principles 3.0 for Effective STEM Philanthropy," undated. As of July 22, 2017: https://www.indianaafterschool.org/wp-content/uploads/2014/09/CTEqDesignPrinciples-STEM -Philanthropy.pdf

———, "Why the State Vital Signs Matter," STEM Vital Signs, 2015. As of July 22, 2018: https://secure.aacte.org/apps/rl/res_get.php?fid=2107&ref=res.

Cornman, Stephen Q., Lei Zhou, Malia R. Howell, and Jumaane Young, *Revenues and Expenditures for Public Elementary and Secondary Education: School Year 2014–15 (Fiscal Year 2015): First Look*, NCES 2018-301. Washington, D.C.: National Center for Education Statistics, 2017. As of July 12, 2018: https://nces.ed.gov/pubs2018/2018301.pdf

Dauphinee, Tom, Alfie McCloud, Wendy Kappy, Richard Howell, and Xin Wang, *Longitudinal Matched-Groups Evaluation of STARBASE New Mexico: Impacts of a DoD Sponsored STEM Program for Fifth and Sixth Grade Students*, Albuquerque, N.M.: University of New Mexico, Center for Education Policy Research, December 2015.

DoD STARBASE—*See* U.S. Department of Defense STARBASE.

Dweck, Carol S., Gregory M. Walton, and Geoffrey L. Cohen, *Academic Tenacity: Mindsets and Skills That Promote Long-Term Learning*, Seattle: Bill & Melinda Gates Foundation, 2014. As of June 17, 2017:
https://ed.stanford.edu/sites/default/files/manual/dweck-walton-cohen-2014.pdf

Ettredge, Michael, John Gerdes, and Gilbert Karuga, "Using Web-Based Search Data to Predict Macroeconomic Statistics," *Communications of the ACM*, Vol. 48, No. 11, November 2005, pp. 87–92.

Getting Started with a LEGO Classroom, undated. As of September 12, 2018:
https://www.cmu.edu/roboticsacademy/roboticscurriculum/Getting%20Started/Lego-Getting -Started.html

Ginsberg, Jeremy, Matthew H. Mohebbi, Rajan S. Patel, Lynnette Brammer, Mark S. Smolinski, and Larry Brilliant, "Detecting Influenza Epidemics Using Search Engine Query Data," *Nature*, Vol. 457, No. 7232, February 19, 2009, pp. 1012–1014.

Google Maps, "The Location of Military Bases in The United States," undated. As of July 10, 2018:
https://www.google.com/maps/d/viewer?mid=1XFBnIuaJ-71hcaDJvdmBmeXNhYM

Grossman, Jean Baldwin, Christianne Lind, Cheryl Hayes, Jennifer McMaken, and Andrew Gersick, *The Cost of Quality Out-of-School-Time Programs*, New York: Wallace Foundation, 2009. As of June 25, 2018:
http://www.wallacefoundation.org/knowledge-center/Documents/The-Cost-of-Quality-of-Out -of-School-Time-Programs.pdf

Jahedi, Salar, Jennie W. Wenger, and Douglas Yeung, *Searching for Information Online: Using Big Data to Identify the Concerns of Potential Army Recruits*, Santa Monica, Calif.: RAND Corporation, RR-1197-A, 2016. As of July 12, 2018:
https://www.rand.org/pubs/research_reports/RR1197.html

Kaplan, Andreas M., and Michael Haenlein. "Users of the World, Unite! The Challenges and Opportunities of Social Media," *Business Horizons*, Vol. 53, No. 1, January–February 2010, pp. 59–68.

Kleykamp, Meredith, "College, Jobs, or the Military? Enlistment During a Time of War," *Social Sciences Quarterly*, Vol. 87, No. 2, June 2006, pp. 272–290.

Korda, Holly, and Zena Itani. "Harnessing Social Media for Health Promotion and Behavior Change," *Health Promotion Practice*, Vol. 14, No. 1, January 2013, pp. 15–23.

Larson, Eric V., personal communication with the authors, October 2017.

Larson, Eric V., Richard E. Darilek, Daniel Gibran, Brian Nichiporuk, Amy Richardson, Lowell H. Schwartz, and Cathryn Quantic Thurston, *Foundations of Effective Influence Operations: A Framework for Enhancing Army Capabilities*, Santa Monica, Calif.: RAND Corporation, MG-654-A, 2009. As of July 10, 2018:
https://www.rand.org/pubs/monographs/MG654.html

Lazer, David, Ryan Kennedy, Gary King, and Alessandro Vespignani, "Big Data. The Parable of Google Flu: Traps in Big Data Analysis," *Science*, Vol. 343, No. 6176, March 14, 2014, pp. 1203–1205.

Legree, Peter J., Paul Gade, Daniel E. Martin, M. A. Fischl, Michael J. Wilson, Veronica Nieva, Rodney A. McCloy, and Janice Laurence, "Military Enlistment and Family Dynamics: Youth and Parental Perspectives," *Military Psychology*, Vol. 12, No. 1, 2000, pp. 31–49.

Margolis, Jane, Rachel Estrella, Joanna Goode, Jennifer Jellison-Holme, and Kim Nao, *Stuck in the Shallow End: Education, Race, and Computing*, Cambridge, Mass.: MIT Press, 2008.

Matsa, Katerina Eva, Amy Mitchell, and Galen Stocking, *Searching for News: The Flint Water Crisis*, Washington, D.C.: Pew Research Center, April 27, 2017. As of July 12, 2018:
http://www.journalism.org/essay/searching-for-news/

Mohr, Caryn, and Dan Mueller, *STARBASE Minnesota Long-Term Follow-Up Study: Overall Results*, Saint Paul, Minn.: Amherst H. Wilder Foundation, July 2012. As of July 10, 2018:
https://www.wilder.org/sites/default/files/imports/StarbaseIII_7-12sum.pdf

National Center for Education Statistics, Common Core of Data, "Data Files," undated. As of July 10, 2018:
https://nces.ed.gov/ccd/ccddata.asp

NCES, CCD—*See* National Center for Education Statistics, Common Core of Data.

Orvis, Bruce, Steven Garber, Philip Hall-Partyka, Christopher E. Maerzluft, and Tiffany Tsai, *Recruiting Strategies to Support the Army's All-Volunteer Force*, Santa Monica, Calif.: RAND Corporation, RR-1211-A, 2016. As of July 10, 2018:
https://www.rand.org/pubs/research_reports/RR1211.html

Perrin, Andrew, *Social Media Usage: 2005–2015*, Washington, D.C.: Pew Research Center, October 8, 2015. As of July 12, 2018:
http://www.pewinternet.org/files/2015/10/PI_2015-10-08_Social-Networking-Usage-2005-2015_FINAL.pdf

Purcell, Kristin, Joanna Brenner, and Lee Rainie, *Search Engine Use 2012*, Washington, D.C.: Pew Research Center, March 9, 2012. As of July 10, 2018:
http://www.pewinternet.org/2012/03/09/search-engine-use-2012/

Quesenberry, Keith A. *Social Media Strategy: Marketing and Advertising in the Consumer Revolution*, Lanham, Md.: Rowman and Littlefield, 2016.

Sharpe Solutions, *Evaluation Report: Low-Cost Randomized Control Trial for Department of Defense STARBASE STEM Program: Museum of Aviation*, Robins Air Force Base, Ga.: Sharpe Solutions, December 2015.

U.S. Air Force, "Find a Recruiter," undated. As of July 12, 2018:
https://www.airforce.com/find-a-recruiter

U.S. Army, "Locate Us: Find a Recruiter," undated. As of July 12, 2018:
http://www.goarmy.com/locate-a-recruiter.html

U.S. Census Bureau, geography landing page, undateda. As of July 26, 2018:
https://www.census.gov/geo/reference/webatlas/divisions.html

U.S. Census Bureau, homepage, undatedb. As of July 10, 2018:
https://www.census.gov

U.S. Department of Defense, Office of the Deputy Assistant Secretary of Defense for Military Community and Family Policy, *2015 Demographics: Profile of the Military Community*, undated. As of July 12, 2018:
http://download.militaryonesource.mil/12038/MOS/Reports/2015-Demographics-Report.pdf

U.S. Department of Defense STARBASE, "Vision and Mission," undated. As of July 10, 2018:
https://dodstarbase.org/vision-and-mission

———, *2014 Annual Report*, Washington, D.C.: U.S. Department of Defense, Office of the Assistant Secretary of Defense for Manpower and Reserve Affairs, 2014.

———, *2015 Annual Report*, Washington, D.C.: U.S. Department of Defense, Office of the Assistant Secretary of Defense for Manpower and Reserve Affairs, 2015.

U.S. Department of Labor, *The STEM Workforce Challenge: The Role of the Public Workforce System in a National Solution for a Competitive Science, Technology, Engineering, and Mathematics (STEM) Workforce*, Washington, D.C.: U.S. Department of Labor, Employment and Training Administration, 2007.

U.S. Navy, "Find Your Navy Recruiter," undated. As of July 12, 2018:
https://www.navy.com/locator.html

Walton, Gregory M., and Geoffrey L. Cohen, "A Question of Belonging: Race, Social Fit, and Achievement," *Journal of Personality and Social Psychology*, Vol. 92, No. 1, 2007, pp. 82–96. As of August 21, 2017:
http://dx.doi.org/10.1037/0022-3514.92.1.82

Welch, Wayne A., "Twenty Years of Science Curriculum: A Look Back," *Review of Research in Education*, Vol. 7, 1979, pp. 282–306.

Wenger, Jennie W., Louay Constant, Linda Cottrell, Thomas E. Trail, Michael J. D. Vermeer, and Stephani L. Wrabel, *National Guard Youth ChalleNGe: Program Progress in 2015–2016*, Santa Monica, Calif.: RAND Corporation, RR-1848-OSD, 2017. As of July 12, 2018:
https://www.rand.org/pubs/research_reports/RR1848.html

Wenger, Jennie W., Jared M. Huff, and Jennifer L. Schulte, "STARBASE: A DoD Program to Increase Interest in STEM Subjects," DRM-2013-U-004082-Final, Arlington, Va.: Center for Naval Analyses, March 2013.